DECEPTION IN THE CHURCH:
THE NEW APOSTOLIC REFORMATION & THE EMERGENT CHURCH

Mumbi Kariuki

DEDICATION

To my children

Faith & Yves Kalala

March 20th 2016

Contents

1

WHAT WOULD IT BE LIKE?

While growing up, I always wondered what it would be like to get to the next level of life. When I was in elementary school, I wondered what it would be like to be in high school. When I was in high school, I wondered what it would be like to be in a university and then what it would be like to have a job, to be married, to have children, to see my children all grown up, or to have grandchildren. With the exception of the last item—grandchildren (and I believe I will have some soon), I went through all these stages and know what it was like.

When the various prophets in the Bible talked about certain things in the Bible, they might have wondered what it would be like. When John the Baptist talked about one who is coming after himself, "the straps of whose sandals" John was "not worthy to stoop down and unloose" (Mark 1:7), he might have thought: I wonder what it will be like when I finally see him? And then, of course, one day when Jesus came, John recognized him and even baptized him. How about Paul, Peter, or Jude when they wrote about the last days? They, too, might have thought to themselves: I wonder what it will be like in those days.

I believe we are living in those days that Paul, Peter, and Jude prophesied and warned about. The days that our Savior Jesus Christ, Son of the Most High God—the creator of heaven and earth, tells us in his Word will precede his Second Coming.

A popular song by Robin Mark states, "These are the days of Elijah . . . these are the days of Ezekiel . . . ." It is a beautiful song especially if you take into consideration Mark's explanation for what motivated him to write the song.[1] However, I mention this song simply to say that if the lyrics were to be written from the perspective of the end times that Jesus, Paul, Peter, and Jude spoke about, one stanza might read as follows:

> These are the days of deception, foretold in the Word of the Lord. These are the days the apostles—Peter, Jude, and Paul foretold. And these are the days that the Lord Jesus himself said would come. We need to watch and pray, pray, for these are perilous times.

The bottom line is that there are many deceivers today who are coming in the name of Jesus. Their goal is to deceive. The chief deceiver is Satan, and he is the one who is the architect of every form of deception that is going on. He is what Revelation 12:9 calls the "great dragon" also known as "that old serpent, called the Devil, and Satan, which deceiveth the whole world."

The Knowing and Unknowing Deceivers

In short, there is the master deceiver Satan, who has created systems of deceptions, and there are people who are being used to operate those systems. The people who operate these systems could be in one of two categories: 1) those who have bought into the deception, they know it is deception, and they are knowingly propagating it and 2) those who have fallen prey to the deception, they have unknowingly bought into the lie, and they are actively but unknowingly propagating the lie.

My heart truly goes out to this second group. Anyone can fall prey to Satan's deception. It is my prayer that God would have mercy and deliver many from this trap, and for this reason that I am putting these words in writing in the hope that someday these words—whether in form of a print book or an e-book—would fall in the hands of one who has fallen prey and is now in danger of not only remaining deceived but also helping to spread the deception.

The Net

I need to use an analogy to help me describe how Satan has set up the deception system. The first idea that comes to mind is fishing. There are many types of fishing nets. Whatever the type, the idea is for the fisherman to go where fish are found, to somehow place the net so that the fish get themselves caught in a way that they cannot escape, and to finally pull the net and the entangled fish out. Put in another way, the fisherman's goal is to get the fish to swim themselves into a location where they cannot escape, "and there! he has them." One such net is known as a drive-in net, which can be described as follows:

It is a dustpan-shaped net, resembling a trawl net with

long wings. The front part of the net is laid along the seabed. The fishermen either wait until a school swims into the net, or they drive fish into it by creating some sort of commotion. Then the net is closed by lifting the front end so the fish cannot escape.[2]

Satan has, as it were, set up a drive-in net and laid it where the unsuspecting targets are. He waits until individuals swim into this net, or sometimes he drives the people into the net using some kind of "commotion." The commotion, for example, could be where one listens to a preacher (maybe at a conference, on a video, on a television program, or in a church setting). The preacher displays some amazing qualities, which he or she attributes to special anointing from God. The listener is then promised, "If you do ABC, you will have the same anointing I have." The listener then tries the A, B, or C not knowing that he or she has just entered into the net from which it is not easy to come out.

Satan has put such drive-in nets in places, and they are catching a great many unsuspecting fish. I think the only variation I can add to this analogy is that unlike a regular fisherman who will want to draw in the net when there are enough fish caught so that he can sell or cook them, in Satan's deception system it may not be in his best interest to quickly draw in the net. The reason is because as soon as the net is pulled out, the fish will soon wake up to the fact that they have been caught as they can no longer breathe or swim freely. Instead, Satan would rather keep his nets in the water until the opportune moment to pull out and not a moment too soon.

It can be said, therefore, that there are many nets that have caught a lot of fish, but the fish have no idea because they can still move about and breathe. There are many people who are deceived but have no idea because things seem relatively normal or, better put, because they are in a lot of close company.

Capture the Flag

Another analogy that comes to mind is the game *capture the flag*. The idea in this game is that each team has a flag and a base. The object of the game is to capture the other team's flag from their base and to deliver it to your own team's base. There are rules, of course, with one of them being that on your way to capturing the flag, you can "paralyze" any of the other team's members by tagging them. This results in their remaining frozen in place for some time and thus unable to defend their territory.

Without going into all the details about the game, I want to borrow the idea of the flag as the prize or the object. When playing this game, you know you are in good shape if you have the other team's flag in your hands. You know you have won the game if you deliver the other team's flag to your own team's base. What does this have to do with Satan's deception system and strategies? The flag is what he hopes for in the end.

The ultimate flag is to destroy everything Jesus Christ stands for. The immediate flag is what he hopes to get true believers in Christ to do now so that he, Satan, can position himself to capture that ultimate flag. He wants to deceive believers into certain practices which will seem, on face value, to be legitimate Christian forms of relating to God but, which if practiced, will lead the same believers to open their lives up to Satan's control. Once he gains this control, he can lead them as a sheep to the slaughter.

This immediate flag is to get you into a practice that will result in you opening your mind to Satan. If he can get you to give him access to your mind, he will gain the kind of control that allows him to accomplish his ultimate plan of deception.

Capture the Waves

Your brain operates at a certain level of activity when it is engaged in thinking or processing thoughts and ideas. However, if you can methodically slow your brain so that it is quiet and not really thinking, the brain switches to a different level. This "not thinking" state that is deliberately and systematically induced is the state that Satan would like you to put your mind in because it is the state in which he is able to take over and give you supernatural experiences.

Take the example of a radio. When you want to listen to your favorite FM or AM radio program, you turn the dial or push the button on your radio receiver (whether a portable radio or the radio in your car). When you hit the right wavelength, you are automatically tuned in to the station and are able to listen into it. Consider the same idea with our human brains. They operate at different states depending on what you are doing. The brain's waves are slowest when in deep sleep and fastest when fully engaged in a mentally challenging activity, such as taking a math test, for example.

Without going into the technical details, suffice it to say that if you induce your brain to a state of not thinking, blankness or emptiness, your brain then can be tuned to the "radio station" where Satan is "broadcasting." Please note that the deceivers will tell you that when you do these things you will be tuned in to God.

There are many ways of inducing this blank mind. These many ways are used by different categories of people who, as part of their culture or religion, have learned to access the supernatural realm. People in these religions and cultures empty their minds or tune to this supernatural realm by engaging in certain types of chanting, dancing, drumming, or different types of yoga. Regardless of the method used, the end goal is to induce a mental state that is receptive to the supernatural.

The most common method of inducing this supernatural-receptive mind state is meditation. This meditation that induces a blank mind is different from the meditation referred to in the Bible, as I will explain later.

In order to deceive Christ's followers into accepting and practicing this mind-blanking meditation, the deceivers have cunningly described, renamed, and presented meditation practices as prayer. The most common name used for this meditation is contemplative prayer. Other names include centering prayer, silent prayer, lectio divina, breath prayers, and soaking prayer.

No matter the name, the idea is the same: to get you to induce your mind into a blankness or an emptiness so that you can slowly tune in to the "station" where the enemy can deceptively speak to your mind and eventually appear to you in some form.

So when you come across, let's say, a book where you are being taught how to practice contemplative prayer, you will be instructed to find a quiet place where you are not likely to encounter any distractions, start breathing and focusing on your inhales and exhales, start repeating a word or phrase, and repeat it over and over again. The breathing slows down your mind while the repeated phrase helps induce the desired state of a blank mind. They will tell you to repeat this regularly—like every morning and every evening for starters, and the more you practice the better you will become at letting go of your thoughts and achieving the desired state. Then they will go into details of what you will experience as you go through the various phases of the exercise.

The goal of this deception is to get you to still your thoughts and stop all conscious thought. The style I have described above, where you find a quiet place, sit, breath, repeat a mantra over and over, is one way they will teach. Another way might include the following: they can suggest you listen to certain types of music and in the music you will be guided into how to quiet and still your thoughts; If you are at a prayer retreat or conference, you might be encouraged to practice this stilling of thoughts as you take a walk. It could be a walk around a building or a parking lot or around a space specifically created for this purpose where you go round a maze-like structure (known as a labyrinth); In the same retreat or conference, you may be taken through guided meditation where the preacher walks you as a group through the breathing, the stilling of thoughts, and the mantra repetition. This group environment could also have music that involves the participants in some form of rigorous chanting, dancing, and quaking—all of which are known to produce the same ultimate result, that of eliminating conscious thought and emptying the mind.

So, let's go back to the analogy of the game of capture the flag. If Satan can get you to practice or be involved in an environment where you learn to induce this blank state of mind, he has captured the flag. If he can get you hooked on it, while somehow believing that it is a legitimate Christian practice, then he wins this part of the game. Of course, if he can get you to start teaching the idea to others, that is a bonus to him.

In upcoming chapters, I hope to get into more detail about what contemplative prayer is and what makes it so dangerous. Indeed, exposing the dangers of contemplative prayer and the various baits that are being used to draw Christians into this net is the strongest motivation behind my writing this book.

Benefit of Doubt

I talked earlier about two categories of people who are being used to propagate Satan's deception: The deceivers (i.e., those who know that what they are teaching is deception) and the deceived (i.e., those who are deceived and do not know but are nevertheless helping to propagate the deception). I repeat this because in the various sections of this book I will mention names (or refer to a website where there are listings) of people who are propagating this deception. I have no way of knowing for sure who is in the first category (a knowing deceiver) and who is in the second (an unknowing deceiver). I hasten to say here that it is fair to give them all the benefit of the doubt and assume they are all in the second category.

What is important is not pinning individuals to one or the other category but rather exposing the deception they are being used to propagate. The idea is to sound the alarm in the hope that some unsuspecting fish will hear and swim away from the dangerous net. In particular, I will be mentioning names of leaders in two main movements: 1) what is generally called the Emergent Church movement (EC) and 2) the New Apostolic Reformation (NAR). These two movements have become like huge drive-in nets. They have caught a lot of fish, and more are being driven into the nets every day. Sadly, most of the fish in the nets or those about to step into the nets have no idea.

That being said, there are many people who have been in these movements, have sensed the danger, have investigated the deception, and are now sounding warnings to believers. At the end of this book, I will provide specific resources that one can explore for further information.

I know that calling these movements deceptive and naming the names of people associated with the movements can seem insensitive or judgmental to some people. However, I believe there is a time and a place for that and I will give you an example. If there were a dangerous loose animal—let's say a sick dog—in your neighborhood, you would want a clear and precise description of this animal so that if you happen to see it from afar, you would be able to take quick action. If it were described as just a dangerous dog, this might leave you exposed to the danger it poses because there are many dogs in your neighborhood. In the same way, these people are posing great danger to unsuspecting believers, and not naming them is choosing to leave these vulnerable believers, some of whom are youth and young children, in danger. As many of the resources provided at the end will show, numerous brothers and sisters have been warning about these false teachings for years.

Heart to heart. As a last thought in this introductory chapter, let me say that I have opted to write this book in a conversational manner. I want it to read like the way I would sound if I were holding a one-on-one conversation with you. In my day job, I do a lot of academic-type writing where almost every sentence has to have one or more citations accompanying it. I could have done that here because I have supporting materials for every claim I am making in this book.

However, one of my goals is to keep this book relatively small to encourage a quick read. If I get it bogged down with details, the book might become too big, and may end up discouraging some potential readers. Do not get me wrong—I love details, and I am one of those who would gladly read a huge book on any topic of interest to me. But there is something about a book that you look at and say, "Oh, I could be done reading that this week or tonight." This is my hope for the readers of my book.

I want to use this book to expose the deception that is happening right now and to do it in a way that hopefully arouses your awareness and invites you to explore and research for yourself. I will know I have been successful in this mission if, at the end of reading this book, you will launch an investigation of your own. To this end, I will provide as many resources as possible as some kind of a starter kit for you. My goal is to do my part in exposing this deception that is infiltrating evangelical churches at an alarming rate.

Once I started understanding this deception, my prayer was that God would help me to share the information with others. Putting this in writing is my attempt to share, and my prayer is that God will put this book into the hands of many who need to read it and that he will lead many into the action he wants them to take thereafter.

Consider what you are reading as my simply relating to you what I have learned after many hours and days of study and research. I am sharing with you in the hope that you can at least investigate the claims I am making and arrive at your own conclusion. If you investigate and find that indeed there is cause for alarm, I would hope and pray that you, too, will pray for a way to share with those who might listen to you just like you have listened to me. I would pray that they too would conduct an investigation of their own, and together we can learn, grow, and beware.

Whatever you do, remember what Jesus said with regard to the end times: "Watch out that no one deceives you" (Matthew 24:4 NIV).

2

COMING TO A CHURCH NEAR YOU

I f your church has not encountered some aspect or another of an attempt to bring in the teachings of the New Apostolic Reformation (NAR) or the Emergent Church (EC), it is one of the few, and likely this attempt is being made or will be made very soon. The future pastor of your church may right now be attending a seminary that is infiltrated by these teachings, and when he comes to you, he will be steeped in the teachings and will slowly steep you in, too. The young people in your church may be attending conferences or missions trips where these teachings are cunningly introduced and followed up in books and other avenues in the media. By attending these conferences and missions trips or reading these books and engaging these materials, the young people are being steeped in these teachings and tomorrow—after all, we like to tell them that they are the future of the church—they will indeed take over, and no one will be any the wiser.

I am not exaggerating. These people (NARs and ECs) are everywhere and spreading quickly.

Apostasy

The Bible speaks about an apostasy or a falling away that will happen in the last days before the second coming of the Lord Jesus Christ (2 Thessalonians 2:3). Apostasy is defined as abandonment of one's religious faith or abandonment of a previous loyalty, which could be a political party, one's principles, or a cause.[1] The word apostasy can also be translated as a defection,[2] which implies a conscious act of abandoning. The apostasy that Paul talked about, then, is an abandonment of the principles of the faith, which Jude describes as the faith that "was once delivered unto the saints" (Jude 1:3).

I believe the teachings of the NAR and EC are resulting in and leading to a massive abandoning of this faith that Jude talked about and urged his readers to contend for. The leaders of these movements (NAR and EC) are being used, knowingly or unknowingly, to propagate a massive deception that is causing many to knowingly or unknowingly abandon the faith of Jesus Christ and follow what Paul called *another Jesus, another spirit,* and *another gospel* (2 Corinthians 11:4) which, by the way, Paul (when talking to the Galatians) said *is no gospel at all* but a distortion of the true gospel of Christ (Galatians 1:6–7 NIV).

Deception

What really is deception? One definition says to deceive is "to cause someone to believe something that is not true, typically in order to gain some personal advantage."[3] Another definition says to deceive is "to cause to accept as true or valid what is false or invalid."[4]

In terms of satanic deception, which is what we are talking about here, the goal of Satan's deception system is to cause believers in Christ Jesus to accept as true what is false in order for him to gain advantage over them. Take, for example, contemplative prayer, which I wrote about in chapter one and will give more details about in upcoming sections. Satan's goal is to get believers to accept contemplative prayer as a true and legitimate way of praying in order for him to deceive them into giving him access to their minds and hence gaining advantage over them and leading them astray. Please note that the NAR and EC are on the forefront of teaching and introducing this deceptive form of prayer, which is really no prayer at all but a distortion of what the Word of God teaches.

Back to the definition of deception and how it is playing out. If you take an example of a building—any building, it starts out with a foundation. Once the foundation is firmly in place, the rest of the building materials are laid according to the plan—the walls, the windows, the doors, the roof and so on—until finally, the finishing touches are applied, and the building is ready for habitation. The deception that is being propagated is similar. The foundation has been established, and the various aspects of building development are taking place. Because the idea is to get you to not recognize the deception for what it is (or else it ceases to be deception), the foundation has been constructed of materials that resemble the truth.

The Deceptive Foundation

I have already indicated that the NAR is an extensive movement that is propagating a massive deception, having laid a deceptive foundation to build on. The deceptive foundation has been: **God is doing something new**. Once you buy into the idea that God is doing something new, then you have taken the first bait, and the rest will follow seamlessly. The big problem here is that the false teachers are the ones who have decided that God is doing something new, and they are the ones who are defining this new thing.

The new thing that God is supposedly doing has been presented in different ways, depending on which of these leaders is doing the presentation. A good example is Chuck Pierce is his book *The Future War of the Church* (coauthored with Rebecca Wagner Sytsema). In this book Pierce describes a vision that God supposedly gave him in 1985. Could this vision have been real? Yes but I should note that I am highly skeptical. In this vision God showed him many things about how the Church is to prepare for the future. He says the Lord showed him that he (the Lord) "would release revelations and gifting for new administrative methods that would cause his people to become influential in the next season of history."[5] He then proceeds to describe how the Lord showed him three upcoming church government structures, which basically leads to the old ways of doing church (or the existing church structure) being replaced by a new one and where the leaders from the existing church would move their offices from the "old building" to the new one, which he calls the *Church of the Future.* [6]

The rest of the book is a detailed account of this new structure that God is putting in place and what we must do to align with what God is doing and how to be part of this *Church of the Future* that Pierce and Sytsema also call the *Third Day Church.* [7]

This Church of the Future, as these authors continue to describe, will have a *new order*. The new order is the new thing that God is instituting. As the authors continue to frame this new thing, they say: "Many in the Body of Christ are referring to the direction the church is taking as the New Apostolic Reformation, a term coined by C. Peter Wagner." [8]

I stop here to note that Chuck Pierce is the current head of the NAR movement, having taken over from C. Peter Wagner in 2010.

According to Wagner, as cited in this same narrative by Pierce and Sytsema, The New Apostolic Reformation (NAR) is a reformation that has been taking place since especially the 1990s and has impacted different aspects of "church life" such as "local church government, interchurch relationships, financing, evangelism, missions, prayer, leadership selection and training, the role of supernatural power, worship, and other important aspects of church life."[9]

If you have been around church life, you will notice that indeed what Wagner is saying in the following statement has been and is happening:

> Some of these changes are being seen within denominations themselves, but for the most part they are taking the form of loosely structured apostolic networks. In virtually every region of the world, these new apostolic churches constitute the fastest growing segment of Christianity.[10]

In this book *The Future War of the Church,* the authors do a great job of laying the foundation of the "new" thing that God is doing. The New Apostolic Reformation is to lead into "a whole new order—new way of doing church."[11] The authors continue to describe how this new but fastest-growing segment of Christianity will be governed and how it will, of necessity, look very different from the way church has been in the past. It is a new order that God is bringing, and it will have:

- A *new authority,* based on a new restoration of the offices of apostles and prophets first, followed by evangelists, teachers, and pastors, all of whom will work together to bring in "the greatest harvest ever to come into the church."[12]
- A *new anointing*, especially for healing, miracles, signs, and wonders.
- *New connections*, which will bring unity based on love for all, knowledge, and vision from the throne room. The key word here is unity—churches coming together and celebrating what they have in common while keeping and maybe even celebrating the different "flavors" they bring.

Armed with this new structure, with the new authority in place, a new anointing leading, and new connections forming every day, the NAR is growing fast, and as I said at the opening paragraph of this chapter, it is coming to a church near you and a city near you if it has not already. Pierce and Sytsema say that this *Third Day Church* is "a building church" for which church planting is a big thing;

"a major part of the building anointing will go toward church planting. The third day church is busy planting networks of churches that will draw in the latter day harvest. The storehouse is being prepared!"[13]

Along with church planting, missions—or sending out missionaries—is also a big part of this new *Third Day Church.* Altogether, entire cities and nations will be transformed as this *Church of the Future* prepares for war and fights with the new weapons or strategies that God is supposedly revealing to these supposed new apostles.

As a reminder, in this section I am discussing how the NAR has defined the new thing that God is supposedly doing (creating the church of the future) and how we are to line up in order to be where God is working. In summary, here is how the deceptive story unfolds: God is doing something new. He is reviving the five-fold ministries in the book of Ephesians 4:11. Therefore, there is a new breed of apostles, prophets, pastors, teachers and evangelists. There is fresh apostolic and prophetic anointing, and God wants us to line up with and tap into this anointing. The apostles are the leaders. They have the apostolic anointing which makes them the vision carriers. The prophets, working closely with and under the apostolic anointing, will lead into the prophetic realms where God will show them by dreams, visions, and special revelations what he is doing and how he wants his people to line up. The pastors, evangelists, and teachers, having submitted themselves under the cover of the apostles and prophets, will spread the message.

Building on the Error-Foundation

Once the foundation is laid, the apostles then get busy casting the vision. They have decided and are deciding what God is doing and how he is going to do it. However, they do not just come out and say I think we should do this or that. No, they get their messages directly from "the source" as they want everyone to believe. Every single one of these apostles has either been to heaven, met with Jesus, and received very specific instructions from him; has had encounters with angels on a regular basis; has had a variety of other supernatural experiences and operates in miracles, signs, and wonders; or has experienced a combination of any or all of the above. Is it possible? Yes. But the more I look into the this movement, the more I doubt that this is truly the case.

I could go into detail and recount how each of the big names in the NAR movement have had these supernatural experiences, but that would take too much space. However, one of the places where these stories abound are on Sid Roth's *Its Supernatural* YouTube Channel. If you search on YouTube any of the names of these leaders (e.g., those listed in chapter 9) plus Sid Roth, you will get the sometimes dramatized versions of these stories. The books these people have written are also full of these stories of supernatural encounters, and as I will mention later, they use these stories to create a sense of hunger and desire in the readers who then quickly fall victim when later introduced to the practice of contemplative prayer-type meditation as a way of gaining intimacy with God. In chapter 5, I will give an example of this from the writings of one of these leaders whose name is Jim Goll.

It is also worth noting here that I am speaking of the NAR as it is today. Historically, the teachings of the movement have taken various shapes and forms and are rooted, for example, in the Latter Rain Movement, which started in the 1940s. Other names of movements that might currently be or have historically been associated with or are synonymous with the NAR include the following: Apostolic Movement, Prophetic Movement, Signs and Wonders Movement, Third Wave, Dominionism, Joel's Army, Manifest Sons of God, and Charismatics.

As it is now and as it has developed, the NAR has different "arms" with different apostles spearheading each, but at the core they have the same ultimate goals and are operating under the same spirit, so to say, as they are in general agreement. The New Apostolic Reformation is some kind of an umbrella name that describes the movement as a whole, and as mentioned above the phrase was coined by one of the chief apostles by the name of C. Peter Wagner. The various apostles and prophets have individual ministries in different corners of the world, but altogether they are knowingly or unknowingly propagating a massive deception. Unfortunately, many Christians have become entangled in these movements.

Warnings

Andrew Strom, once part of the NAR himself, has been warning Christians about the dangers of this movement. I will mention Andrew later in chapter 6, but for now I want to include a statement from one such warning that he issued in 2010.[14] You can access this warning on many web sources by searching "Andrew Strom urgent warning."

Andrew writes:

> Right now I need to do something that I have never done in such a way before. I have never before published a list of ministries or movements to watch out for. But this time I have to. This sickness has gone on long enough. I urge you to cut yourself off from the following ministries and their tainted "anointings," my friends. Even though some of these people say "good things" at times, it is simply not worth having any involvement with them due to the tainted anointing that they endorse or minister in themselves. Here is the list:
>
> (1) Todd Bentley.
> (2) Rodney Howard Browne – the so-called "Holy Ghost Bartender."
> (2) Rick Joyner or anyone connected with Morningstar Ministries.
> (3) John Arnott & any connected with...[Catch the Fire] (the "Toronto Blessing").
> (4) Peter Wagner of the New Apostolic Reformation who claims to be head of a worldwide network of apostle – who publicly endorsed Lakeland and will soon preach at Toronto ...[Catch the Fire] alongside other false anointing advocates.
> (5) Mike Bickle and IHOP Kansas City (I lived nearby for over two years and know how much they are into all this stuff. Mike Bickle promotes it in his book.)
> (6) Bob Jones – the Kansas City prophet whose ministry is utterly tainted by it all.
> (7) Patricia King and anyone else from Extreme

Prophetic.

(8) John Crowder & anyone connected with Sloshfest.

(9) Bill Johnson of Bethel church, Redding – who says some good things but publicly endorsed Lakeland and promotes the false anointing very strongly behind the scenes.

(10) Heidi & Rolland Baker of IRIS Ministries – who do good work amongst the poor in Mozambique but who have also carried and promoted this tainted anointing for years.

(11) Randy Clark, Wes & Stacey Campbell, and other key

figures from the Toronto blessing.

(12) The Elijah List – and almost anyone featured on it.

The leaders named by Andrew in the above list are part of the New Apostolic Reformation. In case you are unfamiliar with Todd Bentley or "Lakeland": Lakeland was a revival primarily featuring Todd Bentley that gained international attention and contained signs, wonders, and very interesting manifestations attributed to the Holy Spirit. In this revival, leaders in the NAR, Peter Wagner, John Arnott, Bill Johnson, Che Ahn, and Rick Joyner, laid hands on, commissioned, and blessed Todd Bentley and the Lakeland Revival for a greater anointing.

Just weeks later, while the revival was still going, Bentley resigned from his ministry and was not able to continue being the speaker at the Lakeland Revival. News came out that Bentley was separating from his wife and that he was in a relationship with a member of his staff. Bentley also had a drinking problem during the revival and after he divorced his wife, married the woman he had been having an affair with.

My Personal Stand

Before I leave this chapter let me clarify where I am coming from in terms of my position on some of the practices I question throughout this book. First is the question of supernatural experiences that many of the leaders especially in the NAR are fond of teaching about. I believe there are two main categories of experiences/events that get labeled as supernatural by believers in general:

a) Experiences/events that are clearly described or outlined in the Bible such as; being filled with the Holy Spirit, being given and operating in any of the spiritual gifts such as those described by Paul in 1 Corinthians 12 and 14, being miraculously healed through laying on of hands and prayer in the name of Jesus as in James 5:14-15 and Mark 16:18. These are genuine Christian supernatural experiences and as long as they are taught and practiced strictly within what the Bible teaches I believe they have their proper place among believers.

b) The second category of supernatural experiences are the types of unusual experiences thought by some to be from God simply because i) even though they are unusual, they are happening in a Christian environment ii) someone claims they are from God, or iii) the original person to have or to introduce such an experience is perceived to be a {very} godly and/or God empowered person. Examples of such experiences are uncontrollable laughter, gold dust appearing on someone's skin, certain types of out-of-body experience, etc. I will call these counterfeit supernatural experiences. In many settings where such supernatural experiences are practiced and/or encouraged they are with time elevated to be of the same status as the genuine ones in a) above. These experiences are presented alongside the genuine ones in such a way that many people are never able to tell the difference and may end up embracing all, indiscriminately.

Some of these unusual experiences such as uncontrollable laughter may be harmless and the individuals involved may even be faking aspects of them. However, others cross the line and become tainted by demonic influences. Examples of these include participating in activities that are meant to induce out-of-body experiences or visible angelic visitations, and so on. I write more about these tainted supernatural experiences in chapter 6.

When I raise concern about any of the supernatural experiences taught, practiced, or embraced by leaders in the NAR or EC I am referring to those that are potentially tainted by demonic influences.

Do I believe that God still performs miracles today? Do I believe in the power of the Holy Spirit working in and among believers through divers spiritual gifts as described by Paul in his letters to the Ephesians (4:11-12), 1 Corinthians chapters 12 and 14, and Romans (12: 6-8)? Do I believe that followers of Christ Jesus can operate according to the words of Jesus in Mark 16: 15-18? The answer is a resounding yes! I am not a cessationist and never have been. In over 35 years of being a Christian I have witnessed the power of God move as believers humbly and reverently submit to the power of the Holy Spirit, as described in the Bible. What I am against is the sneaky introduction of counterfeit supernatural activities and teachings among unsuspecting followers of Christ

Jesus. This book is about highlighting the ways in which this is being done, and the inherent dangers of participating in these counterfeit supernatural experiences, in the hope of sounding a warning. What is of utmost concern to me is that the people teaching these things are telling Christians to get to these supernatural experiences through means which they (the teachers) admit are similar to New Age or Eastern practices, as I will further describe in chapter 7.

In the next chapter, I will describe some elements of the Emergent Church as compared with the NAR. The goal will be to highlight some of the ways you can know whether the persons you may be encountering (as you read a book or listen to a presentation of ideas) are Emergents or NARs. I will also be making the case that though the movements are different in terms of background and general presentation of teachings and ideas, they are also the same in that they are being used to propagate the same deception—that of drawing followers of Christ into the practice of contemplative spirituality.

NAR AND EC: DIFFERENT BUT SAME

The Emergent Church (EC) is another major movement that is drawing young people, in particular, in huge numbers. (See a list of prominent EC leaders in chapter 9). I would say that the NAR is appealing to prospective followers or target groups from the following perspective: a) here is the next move of God which he is revealing to his apostles and prophets through the new anointing he is pouring on them, b) here is how you can join in, and by the way, here are some miracles and signs and wonders to convince you. The Emergent Church, on the other hand, is coming to a prospective target audience from the following perspective: a) here is a new way of understanding God for this age and for our generation, b) we are in a new era, and we must think about what this means with regard to our spirituality, c) this Bible passage does not even mean that . . . or does it, really?, d) come let's explore new ideas of what it really means to be a Christian in this day and age.

The main point I am making in this book is that, despite apparent differences, the chief goal is the same. Like the game of capture the flag I described in chapter 1, the flag that Satan is working to capture through both of these movements is to draw individuals to the practice of mind-blanking activities, which have the potential to grant Satan access to people's minds and hence their lives.

The NAR Teachings and Style

The NAR teachings prey on the sense of hunger and desire for God that many who love Christ and are born again, genuinely feel (and I will revisit this thought in chapter 10). The NAR teachings and style of presentation intensify, in individuals, this feeling of thirst for more of

God, and then they point to deceptive ways to satisfy this hunger and thirst.

If and when you come across an NAR-based environment or teaching whether it be a church, a conference, or media-based materials such as YouTube videos or TV programs, you are likely to encounter, be presented with, or be introduced to practices and ideas such as the ones I have listed below. Another way of stating this is that you will know it is an NAR environment when the practices or ideas and experiences described below are endorsed, embraced, and highly valued as manifestations of the Holy Spirit or encounters with God.

1) Emphasis on the supernatural realm. At the end of chapter two I described what I believe to the different types of supernatural activities, with some being genuine and others being counterfeit. In NAR teachings there is a lot of focus on the supernatural realm and how to access it and as I said earlier this is also the setting where the counterfeit experiences end up being presented, alongside the genuine ones, as though there were no difference.

2) **Being slain in the Spirit.** This is where people are on the floor, some knocked-out unconscious or unable to get on their feet, seemingly held down by some invisible

power. Some of those on the floor may be laughing uncontrollably, writhing, jerking, twitching, or having some other unusual body movements, and some may be producing different types of noises such as groans and animal noises.[1] If you are in the setting for the first time, these things might be quite scary or spooky.[2]

3) **General behaviours.** Worship time might be comprised of people seemingly doing their own thing: some sit on the floor while others jump, dance, or wave hands or flags. Please note that nothing is wrong with these particular forms of expression of worship, I am just stating that these tend to be very common in NAR-based environments. As well, the preacher or speaker will display a variety of theatrics (for lack of a better word). Some, such as Heidi Baker, might on some occasions preach while lying on the floor, supposedly so 'drunk in the spirit' that she cannot maintain an upright position.[3]

4) **Preaching styles.** The speakers may tell many stories about past times when this and that sign, miracle, or wonder happened in such and such a place. The miracles may include what they call creative miracles where new things happen such as instant weight loss, or missing eyeballs restored, people getting instant gold teeth in their

mouths, missing limbs growing out and so on. [3.1]

There may also be stories people being raised from the dead (with most of these resurrections having taken place in some distant part of the world such as in a village in a remote part of Africa where it is impossible to offer proof of death before the reported resurrection). Are things such as healing and raising of the dead possible? Absolutely, but when the people claiming to see such miracles are also having such strange manifestations (attributed to the Holy Spirit), it forces me to think twice before just accepting their testimonies.

The signs and wonders will include strange things like gold dust showing up on people's faces, and things like feathers, clouds and orbs appearing in the room. The stories may also include vivid recollections of supernatural encounters such as visits to heaven, meeting with angels, Jesus or angels appearing in people's rooms and conversing with them, and so on. The speaker might interject various sections of the message to give prophecies or describe visions that God is showing them at the moment. Meanwhile, the speaker will have a variety of bodily movements, such as jerking or shaking, and a variety of noises, such as ooow, whaaaa, aaaw, woooo, interjecting sometimes mid sentences.[4]

5) **Soaking**. Prayer and spiritual warfare will be encouraged, both for private lives and also for groups, which is a good thing. However, soaking prayer will be highlighted as the best way to gain intimacy with God or as some type of a hotline to the throne room of God. Please see my comments about soaking prayer in chapter 4.

These are some of the sights and sounds that one might encounter in a meeting where the NAR teachings and ideas are operating. Any unusual occurrence is attributed to the Holy Spirit's anointing and working. Words or phrases used to describe the various phenomena and experiences include; experiencing the glory, being whacked, wrecked, or undone; moving in the prophetic, and so on.

The Emergent Church Teachings and Style

The EC teachings on the other hand prey on the sense of reason—the innate need in individuals to want to configure, decipher, and understand things as opposed to simply believe. It also preys on the innate need in individuals to want to do something to right the wrongs, evils, and injustices that are in our world—thus making the world a better place is an idea infused in many of the teachings. Similarly, pointing to how the Bible needs to be reinterpreted in order to usher in such a world is the underlying tone of many a message presented in these settings. The process of this need for new understanding calls for questioning, questioning, and more questioning. It also draws on *ancient lost arts* to bring in what is known as *ancient future*, a term used to denote the idea of examining how historical models of spirituality can be applied to the postmodern church of today.

If and when you come across an Emergent Church based environment or teaching, whether it be a church, a conference, or media based materials such as YouTube videos or TV programs, you are likely to encounter, be presented with, or be introduced to practices and ideas such as the following:

1) **The space.** The room may be organized atypically, meaning there will be unusual furniture arrangements. Maybe the pews (if in a church) are removed and replaced by tables organized to create a café-style environment Again please note that there is nothing inherently wrong with atypical furniture organization– I am simply stating a typical feature of an Emergent Church setting. In addition, the room might be darkened and special lighting effects

applied. Among these lighting effects could be candles. The smells in the air might also be different, supplied either by scented candles or burning of some kind of incense. There may also be different prayer stations with icons and items such as beads where participants can go and experience worship using different senses—what they call multisensory worship.

2) **The people.** The speaker may be dressed very casually. He or she may not actually stand in front and speak the whole time. Instead, they may pose a series of questions and encourage the participants to discuss. The mood created will be that of: *Let's ask questions . . . let's explore different explanations or understandings of this or that scripture passage, but bear in mind that we may not ever have an answer.*

3) **The style.** Most of the appeals made in these meetings are bent on convincing the listeners that we are in a new era (postmodern) and that we need to think and act differently and not be held down or back by "misleading" interpretations of the Bible. Everything and anything the Bible says is on the table for questioning, and alternate but "relevant" interpretations are more than welcomed and encouraged. For example, they will pose a question such

as: *Is there really a heaven and a hell that are to come, or is heaven and hell what we are experiencing in the world right now?* This is just an example. Some of the things they will say are not worth repeating because they are very destructive to the way our minds think. At the end of such questioning, many a vulnerable people are left in a state of confusion about what they believe. Often these same people are encouraged to read additional materials, but these materials only lead them further into confusion and away from the simplicity of the Gospel of Jesus Christ.

As an example. An Emergent Church leader by the name of Peter Rollins was invited as one of the main speakers in one youth conference in 2011. I know about this event because youth from my church were in attendance and some of them knew a young lady by the name of Jessie Golem. Inspired by Rollin's teachings, which included among other things the idea that it is okay to doubt your faith, Jessie went on to write a blog entry entitled *"This is why I don't believe in God."*[5] This same blog was later featured in the *Huffington's Post* under the title *"I Was a Hardcore Christian, But This Is Why I Lost My Faith."*[6] Part 1V of the piece, *Nails in the Coffin* is where she explains the encounter with this Emergent speaker, and as Jessie puts it, this encounter was the first nail in the coffin— of the progression of events that led to her losing her faith. Needless to say, despite this story going public in 2012, this same conference has continued to invite key leaders in the Emergent Church movement as main speakers each year. I would hate to think how many times Jessie's story may have been repeated with other young men and women, and who, unlike Jessie, might never blog or otherwise talk about it. I share this story to reiterate my point here that the Emergent Church teachings are potentially lethal to young minds (or any minds for that matter). These teachings are what I would call weapons of mind destruction and we need to shelter our minds and those of our children from such.

4) **Keep questioning and listening, but.** The big idea in an Emergent Church-type environment is to come in with a questioning mind and keep questioning but never think that you or anyone else can tell for sure what the Bible means about any one topic or even whether the Bible is the only authority on the topic. Participants are encouraged to listen to others, regardless of which faith/religious background they come from, and welcome their ideas so that together we can keep the dialogue, which will help us to keep constructing our faith realities and understanding.

5) **Back to the ancient.** When actual teachings are presented, whether in books or speaking forums, they will have a compelling case made of why we need to revisit ancient disciplines and practices whose value has somehow been overlooked. Spiritual formation, silence, the prayer of silence, breath prayers, and a contemplative spirituality will be among these seemingly vintage but certainly new gems for developing a relevant spirituality for today. Speakers like Rob Bell will actually instruct an entire congregation on how to engage in specific breathing exercises as a means of accessing God.[7]

6) **In a nutshell.** In their book *Why We're Not Emergent: By Two Guys Who Should Be*, the authors, Kevin DeYoung, and Ted Kluck provide an interesting to read sentence that I have quoted below:

> You might be an emergent Christian: if you listen to U2, Moby and Johnny Cash's *Hurt* (sometimes in church), use sermon illustrations from *The Sopranos*, drink lattes in the afternoon and Guinness in the evenings, and always use a Mac; if your reading list consists primarily of Stanley Hauerwas, Henri Nouwen, N. T. Wright, Stan Grenz, Dallas Willard, Brennan Manning, Jim Wallis, Frederick Buechner, David Bosch, John Howard Yoder, Wendell Berry, Nancy Murphy, John Franke, Walter

Winks and Lesslie Newbigin (not to mention McLaren, Pagitt, Bell, etc.) and your sparring partners include D. A. Carson, John Calvin, Martyn Lloyd-Jones, and Wayne Grudem; if your idea of quintessential Christian discipleship is Mother Teresa, Martin Luther King Jr., Nelson Mandela, or Desmond Tutu; if you don't like George W. Bush or institutions or big business or capitalism or *Left Behind* Christianity; if your political concerns are poverty, AIDS, imperialism, war-mongering, CEO salaries, consumerism, global warming, racism, and oppression and not so much abortion and gay marriage; if you are into bohemian, goth, rave, or indie; if you talk about the myth of redemptive violence and the myth of certainty; if you lie awake at night having nightmares about all the ways modernism has ruined your life; if you love the Bible as a beautiful, inspiring collection of works that lead us into the mystery of God but is not inerrant; if you search for truth but aren't sure it can be found; if you've ever been to a church with prayer labyrinths, candles, Play-Doh, chalk-drawings, couches, or beanbags (your youth group doesn't count); if you loathe words like *linear, propositional, rational, machine*, and *hierarchy* and use words like *ancient-future, jazz, mosaic, matrix, missional, vintage,* and *dance*; if you grew up in a very conservative Christian home that in retrospect seems legalistic, naïve, and rigid; if you support women in all levels of ministry, prioritize urban over suburban, and like your theology narrative instead of systematic; if you disbelieve in any sacred-secular divide; if you want to be the church and not just go to church; if you long for a community that is relational, tribal, and primal like a river or a garden; if you believe who goes to hell is no one's business and no one may be there anyway; if you believe salvation has a little to do with atoning for guilt and a lot to do with bringing the whole creation back into shalom with its Maker; if you believe following Jesus is not believing the right things but living the right way; if it really bugs you when people talk about going to heaven instead of heaven coming to us; if you disdain monological, didactic preaching; if you use the word 'story' in all your propositions about postmodernism – if all or most of this torturously long sentence describes you, then you might be an emergent Christian [8]

Remember in the current section I am trying to summarize how an Emergent Church based environment, or person for that matter, might look or sound like and the above quote captures this very well. The DeYoung and Kluck book itself is a good read on the topic of Emergents.

The Meeting Point

My argument is that these two movements, (NAR and EC), are working toward the same ultimate goal of luring people into the type of deceptive drive-in fishing nets I described in chapter 1. The idea is to appeal to different categories of people by ultimately bringing them to the practice of tuning in to the supernatural realm where Satan is able to deceptively take control of individuals. The message I am trying to highlight in this book is that getting Christians to entertain and explore practices that will lead individuals to access the supernatural realm, using satanic means but all the while being duped into thinking it is the new thing God is revealing about himself, is the ultimate goal of Satan's deception and hence the goal of these deceptive movements.

Once an individual starts accessing this supernatural realm through the practicing of contemplative prayer type-meditation, for example, the rest takes care of itself or, better put, the devil has seen to it that the rest will take care of itself as described in the next paragraph.

The practice of blanking out your mind through meditation or other means opens your mind up to the spirit world. Once you gain contact and communication with these spirits, they will guide the rest of the show. Of course, they will not come to you and say, "Hi, I am an evil spirit, and I want to enter your body and be leading you from within from now on." No, these spirits are of Satan—the master deceiver. They will operate deceptively. They will pretend to be what it is you are searching for, hungry for, or desperate for. Are you desperate for an encounter with the supernatural? Then they will lead you to one. Do you want to see Jesus? They will pretend to be Jesus and will speak like you would expect Jesus to speak. Do you want to go to heaven? Sure, that can be arranged. There is a practice called astral projection, which can allow your spirit body to leave your physical body, go to the supernatural realm, and see things. Of course, this is an occult practice, but the demons will not tell you that . . . and the false teachers who invite you into these practices will not tell you that. When these people describe their visit to heaven or their other encounters with the supernatural, they do it in such a way that by the time you are done listening to them, you strongly desire to go there too, or to have similar experiences.

As I mentioned earlier, many people in the world practice meditation. It is an integral teaching of the New Age movement, Hinduism, and Buddhism, among others. The blank-your-mind-type of meditation is the practice by which witches and psychics gain access to the supernatural realm.

It is not a new thing. What is new is trying to get evangelical Christians to join in, and that is what these movements—that are coming to a church near you are doing, slowly but surely.

4

CONTEMPLATIVE PRAYER

ontemplative prayer is a form of meditation. Meditation, as I have already mentioned, is not a new idea. It has been practiced for centuries by many religions and cultures throughout the world. One of the baits that is used to draw Christians into meditation is that it is presented by the deceivers as a biblical practice. What the deceivers do not tell you is that there is a huge difference between meditation as described in the Bible and the meditation implied in contemplative prayer. The fact that many people do not know the difference is the bait the deceivers use to lure people into the practice of contemplative prayer.

Meditation in the Bible. In the Bible meditation is an active pondering of what God's Word says. When you meditate on the Word of God, you think about it . . . you actively ponder on, whether it is the meaning or implication of a phrase in the section you are reading or an attribute of God as described in the section. You keep your mind alert to the thoughts going through it. Indeed, you keep charge of your thoughts.

Meditation as practiced by Buddhists, New Agers, etc. In this kind of meditation, the key, the goal, and the object are to empty one's mind using one of many techniques. It is an empty-your-mind kind of meditation. Contemplative prayer is meditation in this category.

There is no place in the Bible where we are required or encouraged to empty our minds. Contemplative prayer is not prayer, and it is not biblical. However, for something to be deceptive it has to look and sound legitimate to the victim. One of the favorite verses used to justify contemplative prayer is Psalm 46:10 which states: "Be still, and know that I am God." However, this verse is not about how to pray. It is about resting in God as opposed to fretting. The full verse states, "Be still, and know that I am God: I will be exalted among the heathen, I will be exalted in the earth." If you look at the entire Psalm (46), you will see that the context of it is not how to go before God, but rather how to rest in God as your refuge and present help.

Another passage that is used to justify contemplative prayer is Mathew 6:6 (NIV) where Jesus said, "But when you pray, go into your room, close the door and pray to your Father who is unseen. Then your Father, who sees what is done in secret, will reward you." These teachers will say that closing the door is equivalent to shutting off your distracting thoughts, and they will then continue to teach the rest of the contemplative prayer process, sometimes including the repeating a word or a phrase (aka a mantra).

However, if you look at the context of what Jesus was saying in Mathew 6:1–18 (please read), it is about our attitude when we do acts of service or worship to God. He is teaching that we should do such acts not for show, but rather in secret to God because he can see in secret and reward us accordingly. Jesus says, for example, when you give to the poor, do not announce it with trumpets as hypocrites do (verse 2); and when you fast, do not allow your physical appearance to show that you are fasting (verses 16–18). So it is within this same context that Jesus says when you pray, do not do it like the hypocrites who love to stand in places where people can see for sure that they are praying. Instead, go into your room, close the door, and pray to your Father who will see and hear even though others cannot see and hear you. This going into your room and closing the door implies that prayer is something between you and God and not a show-off activity.

While on this section of scripture, please note Matthew 6:7) where Jesus said, "But when ye pray, use not vain repetitions, as the heathen do: for they think that they shall be heard for their much speaking." Jesus warned against using vain repetitions. The special word they say to repeat over and over and over is a perfect example of vain repetition, wouldn't you say? The very passage these people misuse to justify contemplative prayer is actually the passage that warns against it.

Let me insert another thought here. When one wants to study a topic from the Bible, the right thing to do is to pull together all the scripture passages that allude to the topic and consider them together. In this case with the topic being prayer, the right thing to do would be to take all the passages that teach about prayer and see what they are altogether teaching. In reality, prayer in the Bible is not a passive practice. It involves asking, beseeching God, making requests known, supplicating, and petitioning—all of which are very active processes.

The truth is that contemplative prayer is designed to get you to open your mind so as to gain contact with the spirit world. Once you gain this contact, you will meet angels—except they will not be holy angels but evil angels (aka, demons). These demons will pretend to be God's angels. They will speak and behave in such a way that you will think they are holy angels after which they will deceptively get you to follow their advice and to depend on them for more. All this time you will be thinking that you are having a special spiritual experience or an encounter with God, and you will crave for more.

The bottom line is that Satan is out to deceive. He wants to deceive the whole world so that in the end he can get the worship he has craved for ever since he rebelled against God. He has a plan. The plan is simple: If he can get you to practice blanking your mind in the name of prayer, he can write the rest of the story. All he needs is for you to practice contemplative prayer.

Contemplative prayer, which is also often referred to as centering prayer, is meditation with occult roots. It is presented so as to look like a legitimate spiritual activity for Christians; however, it is highly dangerous, and we must run away even from the appearance of it because it is evil. Its roots are satanic. Getting you to practice contemplative prayer is Satan's chief goal and last-ditch effort to deceive you. You inducing your mind to a blank state is the flag he wants to capture. As Ray Yugren says, "Unknown to most people, a blank mind in a meditative state is all that is necessary for contact with a spirit guide."[1] (Spirit guides are actually demonic spirits who masquerade as helpers in order to trap and destroy people with false teachings and occult practices.[2])

Matt Slick, from Christian Apologetics and Research Ministry (CARM) says the following:

> Before I became a Christian, I was involved in the occult. One of the practices I would undergo when trying to contact the spiritual realm and/or trying to receive some mystical experience would be to empty my mind, remain motionless, and completely open

myself up to receive whatever would come. Essentially, I was seeking an altered state of consciousness and contact with the spiritual world. This is one of the hallmarks of occultic practices, and it opens the person to demonic contact.

This centering, this emptying of the mind was a physical and mental process of stillness, waiting, non-thinking, and expecting to have a spiritual experience. It worked. Using these techniques, I have seen lights move in darkness, a bright yellow cross materialize out of thin air, and I've heard voices calling me from the darkness. I'm not exaggerating. I was not on drugs, medicated, drinking, or sleep deprived. I definitely contacted something in the spirit realm. But, it wasn't God.[3]

Let us not ignore the warnings that are being sounded. I write this with much heaviness in my heart because all of my Christian life I have desired to learn as much as I can about serving and loving God with all my heart. I have read many books by Christian authors, and many have helped and encouraged me in my walk of faith. But as I will share later, many of the books available for such reading today are by these deceptive authors, and I know how easy it is to fall prey to these teachings because these authors make convincing presentations in their writings. I have books in my home library that I started to read only to realize that they somehow did not line up with what I know the Bible says, and it is not until I started piecing together how this deception is happening that I now understand why those books were not lining up for me. Unfortunately, not every person who is reading these books, attending conferences, or watching these teachings on TV or other media will quickly sense the deception.

A Word About Soaking Prayer

It used to be you soaked clothes before washing them or soaked beans overnight before boiling them, but the word soaking has taken on another meaning in the recent past. If you are or know someone who is associated with the Toronto Catch the Fire Church, Bethel Church in Redding California, IHOP, Iris Global, MorningStar Ministries, and other similar ministries, then you would have heard of or practiced soaking as a form of prayer. The idea behind soaking is to sit or lie down in a quiet place, play some music, and just silently listen—no talking, no singing along, just quietly listen. Most people think: *Well, what could be wrong with that?* The truth is that "soaking prayer is a modern form of contemplative prayer."[4] Soaking prayer is a form of meditation and may lead to a blanking of the mind, which will then lead to tuning in to the evil spirit realm as discussed throughout this book.

In the February 2001 issue of *Spread The Fire Revival Magazine*,[5] a number of leaders talk/teach about soaking prayer under articles with different titles such as Carol Arnott's "The Purpose of Soaking in His Love," Dawn Critchley's "Finding My Place of Rest," Heidi Baker's "Soaking in His Presence Ministering to the Poor," and Jim Goll's "The Pathway to More of Him." There is also a piece written by Mark Virkler entitled "Soaking for Left Brainers." It is clear from reading these articles that the authors see soaking as a form of, or as synonymous with, contemplative prayer. Goll, for example, makes reference to "the spiritual consolation you will receive from direct contact with the Holy Spirit during times of contemplative or soaking prayer . . ."[6] Jim Goll's article in this issue seems to come almost verbatim from his book *The Lost Art of Practicing His Presence* where he teaches contemplative prayer in depth. (I will say more about this book in chapter 5).

Mark Virkler is a much-sought-after speaker and voice on how to hear from God. He describes how he desired to know how to hear God's voice and how, after much searching without success, he finally took a year off to learn to hear God's voice. During this time off, he read every book he could find, went to every conference he could find, read the Bible, experimented, asked people, and finally God synthesized the whole thing for him into four simple steps: still your thoughts, fix your eyes on Jesus, tune into spontaneity, and journal.[7]

According to Virkler, soaking is a way to still your thoughts. Virkler's four steps therefore essentially entail: 1) start {the process of contemplative prayer through} soaking, 2) enter into visualization (i.e., visualize Jesus), 3) expect to hear or see something spontaneously, and 4) journal because what you hear will be Jesus talking to you. However, if a New Ager or a psychic engaged in something similar, it would be exactly the same, except for reference on Jesus or God. It would be something like 1) start meditation, 2) enter into visualization to activate your psychic abilities or your third eye, 3) your spirit guide or other Being will speak to you spontaneously, and 4) start journaling whatever the spirit guide or other Beings tell you.

This practice of tuning to the spirit world and writing what you hear coming to you is called channeling in occult language.

I believe what Virkler is teaching to thousands of Christians who are hungering to hear from God is an occult practice. Sure, it will lead people to hear and see things, but these things will not be of God.

> "Visualization" and "Guided Imagery" have long been recognized by sorcerers of all kinds as the most powerful and effective methodology for contacting the spirit world in order to acquire supernatural power, knowledge, and healing. Such methods are neither taught or practiced in the Bible as helps to faith or prayer.[8]

My dear reader, stay away from soaking prayer no matter who is teaching it and stay away from any element of visualization no matter who is teaching it or what it is called. These are occult practices coated with a Christian flavor. Instead, when you want to pray, come to God by faith and make your requests known to him with supplications and thanksgiving. Ask, keep on asking, and do not give up. God will answer your prayer. Remember to forgive and repent as you approach God. Your faith in him and his Word is all he wants from you. You do not need to visualize anything. If you make a practice of visualization and stilling your thoughts, you are playing with fire, as these are occult practices, and they work—only they will lead you to another Jesus and another spirit, deceiving you.

This is dangerous stuff.

In the next chapter, I will focus on how contemplative prayer is introduced to Christians. In particular, I will look at some books where this is taught.

Children and Youth

But before I leave this chapter, let me also mention that one of the greatest concerns is that these practices of contemplative spirituality—whether centering prayer or soaking prayer—are being taught to children and youth, and many parents are not aware either because the parents do not know the dangers yet or because the teachings take place away from the parents' sights. Youth conferences, youth reading materials, and other youth-based media—to say nothing of church-based youth groups and Sunday school classes—are all avenues for introducing contemplative prayer to the young.

If you go to your church library, you will probably find a book by Mark Yaconelli. If not, ask a few young Christians, and it will not be long before you find someone who has heard of Yaconelli. That is because Yaconelli is a well-known teacher on youth ministry. Mark openly teaches contemplative spirituality to youth leaders and youth.

In the above mentioned February 2001 issue of *Spread The Fire Revival Magazine*, Heidi Baker makes the following statement:

> Rolland and I teach the children in our orphanage to soak in God's presence, too. We ask them to lie down and wait for Jesus. There have been several meetings where the divine presence of the Lord has come and no one could stand. The children began to see visions. One little girl saw a big, white cross in the prayer hut. Another little boy saw a lake of fire, and then he saw Jesus take him by the hand, and they leapt over the fire and stood on the other side. Children who were once severely abused often see God lifting them up to sit on His lap.[9]

If contemplative prayer is wrong for Christians because it induces a blank mind that creates connections to the evil spirit world, and if soaking is contemplative prayer, then indeed people like Heidi and Rolland Baker, and those working for them or under them or following their example, are introducing these children to practices that will open them up to this evil spirit realm. Heidi and Rolland may be doing an admirable job of feeding the children and providing them with basic as well as life-changing opportunities; however, if at the same time they are leading the children to veiled occult practices in the name of prayer and intimacy with God, I can only hope (for their own sake) that they are doing this unknowingly.

The matter of children being taught this stuff is extremely saddening.

ARE YOU HUNGRY FOR GOD?

any believers are hungry and thirsty for more of God. I do not know of many Christians who would not want to know God better, have more spiritual insight, pray more effectively, see God in their day-to-day activities, and hear God's voice speaking to them in specific terms. This desire becomes even more deeper when you encounter people who claim to have "been there and done that"—you know, they have seen Jesus, visited heaven, angels have visited them and talked to them, God talks to them every day, they see miracles every day when they pray, and so on.

It is very easy to be drawn in by any such stories and find yourself desperate for God, or described another way, desperate for these kinds of experiences. You may find yourself reading the books written by or watching videos prepared by these people, and there are plenty of them. The videos and books describe in vivid detail how these experiences happen. Some of the books also offer "how to" sections and encourage you to try various ideas. The ideas may include fast more often, go for a mission, and so on, but most importantly, pray. Sounds good so far, but the trick lies in what kind of prayer they ask you to pray, and this is often how contemplative prayer is introduced.

I will give you an example of one such book: *The Seer; The Prophetic Power of Visions, Dreams and Open Heaven* (2004).[1] The point I want to make here is that the author spends most of the book introducing the reader to amazing possibilities in terms of developing intimacy with God—all the wonderful supernatural experiences one could have—and then eventually suggests contemplative prayer as the way to attain these supernatural experiences.

In this book the author, Jim Goll, who is one of the most prominent teachers on contemplative prayer, by the way, describes to the reader what it means to operate in the seer realm.

In the first section he describes the seer realm, explaining the difference between a seer and a prophet and naming different leaders who are operating in the various realms. For example, dreamers and visionaries (or the seers) are those "who move primarily in the realm of dreams and visions"[2] and Bob Jones, Paul Cain, and John Paul Jackson, are named as specific modern day examples.[3] Down the list of various dimensions of prophetic anointing, Goll names others such as Rick Joyner, Bill Hammon, Francis Frangipane, Tommy Teeney, Norm Stone, Scott Macleod, Jason Upton, David Ruis, Heather Clark, Cindy Jacobs, Chuck Pierce, Jill Austin, John and Paul Sandford, John Wimber, Mahesh and Bonnie Chavda, Patricia King, and Todd Bentley, among others.[4]

The rest of the book teaches much about what one

needs to know about these two streams—the prophetic and the seer.

For those who are hungry for this kind of stuff and are seeking to get a grasp on the topic, the book is indeed very informational, but in my assessment, having read this book, I would place it in the "dangerous books" category. In section three of the book, Goll gives information about "dreams, visions, and other heavenly realms." He opens chapter 7 with the statement, "Generally speaking, the Holy Spirit uses three different avenues of visionary revelation to speak into our lives: dreams, visions, and trances.⁵ So, in chapter 7, 8, and 9, Goll provides insights into these three avenues, describing different types of dreams and how to interpret the symbolism in dreams, different types of visions, and trances.

Out-of-body experiences. Of particular interest is where he mentions out-of-body experiences and heavenly visitations as examples of visions:

> *An out-of-body experience is the actual projecting of a person's spirit from his or her body. When God inspires such an experience, he puts a special faith, anointing, and or protection around the person's spirit so that*

he or she can perform in the arena when the Lord is leading. In an out-of-body experience, a person's spirit literally leaves his or her physical body and begins to travel in the spiritual dimension by the Spirit of the Lord. Once out there the surrounding environment appears different than it does naturally because now the spiritual eyes are seeing not the natural eyes. The Lord directs the eyes to see what he wants them to see in exactly the way he wants them to see it. [6]

Before I proceed, let me point out that if a Hindu Yoga practitioner was to describe an out-of-body experience, they would probably use the same wording but replace the words God, Spirit, and the Lord with other terms like a Higher Being or spirit guide. What Goll is describing is a practice rooted in the occult, but he is using Christian terms to make it sound biblical. Ironically, Goll adds that we must be very careful about an out-of-body experience "because of its occultic association in the mind of many people"[7] He admits that sorcerers and yogis practice something similar, but he says when it is God-initiated it is okay. He ends this section with the exhortation: "Do not let the enemy steal what God has ordained. Do not be afraid of these unusual ways of the Holy Spirit and yet do not enter into some self-induced activity."[8] Please understand, as a believers we should be extremely cautious when approaching these what Goll is calling "unusual ways of the Holy Spirit" type of experiences, particularly because Goll's method for entering into these experiences is without a doubt rooted in the occult.

Heavenly visitations. The other equally unusual type of vision as described by Goll is "heavenly vision," which is "like an out-of-body experience" except that the person's spirit leaves the earth realm, passes through the second heaven, and goes to the third heaven. This can occur while the person is praying, while in a trance or deep sleep from the Lord or at death.[9] He ends this discussion on visions by saying that:

> I believe heavenly visitations have occurred not only in the Bible but throughout history, and that such experiences will increase as true prophetic ministry emerges in these last days. Join me and express your desire that you might step into all that our Father God has prepared for you.[10]

The desire for a heavenly visitations is not wrong in and of itself. The means by which Goll teaches we can obtain this desire, however, is very wrong. Goll is about to introduce you to contemplative prayer as the way to activate these experiences.

Swallow the bait? This, therefore, brings me to the part of the book that made me suggest it as an example of how contemplative prayer is introduced, taught, and encouraged. Goll, as I have summarized above, teaches on how amazing these experiences (dreams visions, trances, etc.) are, citing different examples of people who have enjoyed this "special anointing" and encouraging the reader to desire the same. From the presentations in sections 1–3 in the book, he does a good job of making the reader want more, be desperate, and be hungry for all that God has in store. At the end of Chapter 3, which is on visions, he encourages the reader with the following words:

> *What is the Lord calling on your life? Ask Him to give you a vision of it and don't stop asking, Keep on looking until you see it . . . Ask that a revelatory shaft of light would enter your spirit so that you would know the hope and the expectation of good for your life . . .* [11]

Let me pause here to beg you to not look for a vision because the Bible does not tell us to look for a vision. Whatever you do, do not ask for a *revelatory shaft of light* to enter your spirit. The Bible says nothing about a revelatory shaft of light, so do not ask for it. *"Shaft of light"* is occult language.

All throughout Goll's book the reader is drawn in or lured toward amazing possibilities of intimacy with God—the kind that is made possible by operating in the realms of the supernatural as described in the book. In chapter 11, Goll comes to the climax of his writing with the following words:

> *In my own experience I have found that the most direct road to greater intimacy with God has come through the practice of a discipline of an almost lost art in the fast pace church of today— something called contemplative prayer. Since discovering it well over a decade ago, it has become one of my loves, one of the central features of my walk with God.*[12]

Goll proceeds to describe his experience with contemplative prayer and finally describes the three phases that one would go through when engaging in the type of contemplative prayer he teaches: Phase one *recollection,* where you "put away all obstacles of the heart, all distractions of the mind and all vacillations of the will," is followed by phase two, *prayer of quiet,* where:

> *divine graces of love and adoration wash over us like ocean waves and at the center of our being, we are*

hushed, and there is a stillness, to be sure, but it is a listening stillness. Something deep inside of us has been awakened and brought to attention, and our spirit is now on tiptoe alert and listening. Then comes out an inward steady gaze of the heat sometimes called "beholding the Lord."[13]

Goll finally describes the third and final phase of a contemplative prayer experience as *spiritual ecstasy,* which is a "place of quiet detachment" from reality, where "illumination—the spirit of revelation is granted" and one's "being becomes filled with God's pictures, God's thoughts, and God's heart."[14]

This stuff—the experience of contemplative prayer and the various ways it can be done and the various stages—is not in the Bible. Those who know what happens through the various stages know it from having experienced it rather than from the Bible. Unfortunately, these experiences are very similar to those of occult practitioners and Hindu gurus and yogis who practice meditation. The only difference between the two sets of parallel experiences is the words and phrases. The Christian practitioners like Goll will use "God" and "Holy Spirit" while the occult-based practitioners will not.

Jim Goll, who is clearly part of the NAR, is one of the most vocal or in-the-front proponents and teachers of contemplative prayer. I gave an example of the book *The Seer* above as an example of how he builds the reader to desire dreams, visions, and intimacy with God and then finally introduces contemplative prayer as the fastest way of getting this intimacy. His next book *The Lost Art of Practicing His Presence*[15] is a downright, all-out teaching of contemplative prayer. As though to continue where the Seer book ends, Goll says the following:

> Many Christians today, although desperately hungry for intimacy with God, get nervous at the mention of words like contemplation, meditation, centering and quietness (not to mention the ugly word discipline) because of their modern association with the occult, Eastern mysticism, and New Age.[16]

First, let me stop here to say, Yes, "many Christians today although desperately hungry for intimacy with God [should be very] nervous at the mention of words like contemplation, meditation, and centering and quietness... [precisely] because of their modern association with the occult, Eastern mysticism, and New Age." Indeed, that is the whole point of this book. We should not only be nervous, but those who can should research and know the facts and those who can should warn the rest, and all of us should flee from this like we would from a dangerous plague.

I said earlier that I would like to keep this book short to encourage a quick read, so I will not go into more depth or exploration of Goll's teaching on this contemplative prayer practice, which is what he calls a *lost art* that he (and others) are now reintroducing back to us as a legitimate and time-honored method of drawing near to God. I will, however, mention Goll once more in Chapter 8 when I discuss how he and others claim that these practices were stolen by the occult practitioners and that we need to reclaim them. My argument and suggestion to you is that we have nothing to reclaim from the enemy.

Modes of Presentation

The experiences and practices that lead to opening oneself to the supernatural are presented to Christians in any number of ways. As I mentioned in chapter 1, you may find yourself in a meeting where you are being led into a group-based, guided prayer on how to let go of your thoughts, followed by how to say a word repeatedly, whether the word is in the form of a song, or a chant. You may be listening to recorded instructions, whether a teaching video or a song, and again you are guided into how to do these things alone. You could also be reading a book similar to the example of Jim Goll's books I have referenced above.

The book you may be reading or video or person you may be listening to may use certain names to describe the practice being taught. Many will teach and call it contemplative prayer. Other ways of describing the practice are centering prayer, silent prayer, lectio divina, spiritual formation, prayer of the heart, and soaking prayer, among others. The person writing or talking may use words or phrases such as going to the secret place with God, practicing his Presence, moving into the holy place, entering into intimacy with God (or Abba), entering the glory realm, and so on.

Whatever the deceptive practice is named or whichever way they lead you to the practice, the goal is the same: to get you to zone out of your conscious thoughts and to empty your mind thereby giving evil spirits access to your mind and thoughts. The evil spirits will take over and speak to you and guide you in ways that deceive you into thinking that you are communing with and being led by the Holy Spirit or by angels. This will draw you further into the practice, leading to more levels of "intimacy" and "revelations," all from Satan but deceptively designed so you think you are gaining more intimacy with, and getting more revelations and encounters from, God.

Real But Not True

Also worth noting here is that the results of contemplative prayer are real. If you practice contemplative prayer, you will feel something, see something, hear something, and go places. The experiences may even be pleasant and seemingly authentic—enough to get you hooked on the practice eventually. The fact that these experiences are real not fake is the greatest concern. The "angels" you will see will actually be demons. The "Jesus" who will talk to you or you will see will be a demon masquerading as an angel of light. The "heaven" you will go to will be an evil spirit world masqueraded to look like what you might expect to see if you were to actually go to the real heaven. The miracles, signs, and wonders you will see are real, except from Satan who the Bible says works signs and lying wonders (2 Thessalonians 2:9).

Others and I are not sounding a warning because these things are fake. Indeed, it is because these practices lead to real but deceptive and satanic experiences that make them all the more dangerous.

One of the dangers of meditation for a Christian is the possibility of what is commonly known in Hinduism as kundalini awakening. In the next chapter I will discuss this phenomenon and how it has manifested itself in Christian circles.

KUNDALINI AWAKENING

Since the early 1990s, a new phenomenon has emerged that has taken over many charismatic gatherings. One of the examples of this phenomenon started in Toronto and is commonly known as the Toronto Blessing. In this event, Randy Clark was invited by John Arnott to what was then the Toronto Vineyard Church. Randy had previously received an "anointing" from Rodney

Howard-Browne. In a "revival" that lasted over ninety days, Clark laid hands on the participants who received the "anointing," which included being knocked out of consciousness (they call it slain in the spirit), people making a variety of animal sounds (a dog *bark, bark* over here, a wolf *woof, woof* over there, a pig *oink, oink* on this corner, and a lion *growl, growl* in the other corner), trembling, shaking, laughing uncontrollably for long periods of time, feeling of warmth and cold in the body, emotional outbursts such as crying and weeping, jerking movements, strange postures, drunken-like states, and new revelations. Read the following description as described on their own Catch the Fire website:

> The Toronto Blessing is a transferable anointing. In its most visible form it overcomes worshippers with outbreaks of laughter, weeping, groaning, shaking, falling, "drunkenness," and even behaviors that have been described as a "cross between a jungle and a farmyard."[1]

This "anointing" has spread to many parts of the world. As continued on the same Catch the Fire website:

> The "Toronto Blessing" has spread, not only to England, but to Switzerland, Germany, Hungary, Norway, Finland, Holland, Japan, South Africa,

Zimbabwe, Korea, India, Taiwan, Thailand, Guyana (South America), Cambodia, Australia, New Zealand, Indonesia, Malaysia, Singapore, Czechoslavakia, Russia, mainland China, Denmark, Iceland, Sweden, Romania, New Guinea, Kenya, Israel, and many other places.[2]

The author of an article on the Toronto Blessing (TB) gave the following account:

> Almost all the spiritual phenomena and experiences which are now called the TB were in fact already taking place under the ministries of men like Benny Hinn, Rodney Howard-Browne, and Kenneth Copeland years before the Toronto Airport Vineyard Church took these things on board. I've especially singled out these three men because it was Rodney Howard-Browne who transmitted the blessing or anointing to the Toronto Airport Vineyard, and Howard-Browne has been closely linked with the ministries of Benny Hinn and Kenneth Copeland.[3]

I quote this statement because many people have watched Benny Hinn perform on TV and maybe have wondered much about him but did not know what to make of his style of performance. I believe the same phenomenon that is in the Toronto Blessing is in operation in many ministries, including that of Mr. Hinn.

Kundalini Parallel

While there is no parallel of this Toronto Blessing experience in the Bible, a parallel experience exists that happens in people who practice kundalini yoga and various types of mind-blanking activities.

In Hinduism it is believed that there is energy coiled in the shape of a serpent at the base of the spine. This energy can be awakened and when this happens, the energy moves up the spine through seven different areas (more like pools of energy known as chakras) all the way to the top of the head. When this awakening happens, it produces certain effects in the individual such as the following: a feeling of warmth or cold, joy, tingling, waves of bliss, animal sounds, involuntary jerks, shaking, and a crawling sensation especially in the limbs. The manifestations in the Toronto Blessing and those by kundalini yoga practitioners are virtually identical.[4]

This kundalini energy can be awakened spontaneously by 1) laying on of hands by one who has had the awakening themselves, or 2) through meditation (which includes contemplative prayer and its various forms such as centering prayer and soaking prayer). It is noted "a short cut to an awakened kundalini is through a Guru or so called holy man"[5]. However, it is also the case that this kundalini energy is contagious and being in the presence of someone "who is already on fire" can cause a spontaneous awakening to those around such a person.[6]

Those who practice or experts in kundalini awakening warn that spontaneous awakenings can be dangerous and can cause adverse negatives effects such as depression, heart palpitations, strange illnesses, and "radical mental, emotional, interpersonal, psychic, spiritual, and lifestyle changes."[7] The same experts insist that an awakening should be done under the supervision of an experienced teacher who would counsel on how to handle the energy in order to avoid the extreme side effects. I mention this here for two reasons: 1) to highlight the fact that even those who practice this as part of their culture/religion warn of possible dangers and 2) to remind that if Christians get this awakening (disguised as a legit touch from God), they are not exempt from the dangers. Indeed, there are scores of Christians who have experienced these spontaneous awakenings, are dealing with these negatives effects, and are warning people about these dangers.

Andrew Strom has spoken and written extensively on this kundalini phenomenon as it relates to the deception is has brought in the church of Jesus Christ. In his book *Kundalini Warning: Are False Spirits Invading the Church,* he describes this invasion and gives several examples of individuals who were affected in various ways. This book is a highly recommended read for anyone who wants to understand this phenomenon.[8] Andrew also has a YouTube video where he shows the similarities between kundalini-based manifestations as practiced by kundalini cults and what has been happening in the Toronto Blessing-based manifestations.[8.1]

What is extremely sad is that many Christians have flocked into churches and meetings that have these kundalini-type manifestations and have subjected themselves to the laying of hands from people who may very well be imparting kundalini energy to them. There is no way of knowing how many Christians are struggling with the after effects—the strange experiences in their bodies—and wondering what to do but all the while convinced that God is doing a work in them.

How many people have laid on the floor unconscious, meanwhile have had visions of angels (who are really demons masquerading as angels), and all the while they were supposedly "slain in the spirit" and getting a healing from childhood hurts? How many Christians have laid on a floor writhing, contorted and too giddy to rise up or stand on their own, which are typical kundalini symptoms, but all the while are envied by those around them because they are having an "encounter with God" and they are "drunk in the spirit."

Many of these people have gone home to start a new life of strange experiences. Some of these experiences are so strange that they do not exactly wish to, or know how to, share with others such as "intensified or diminished sexual desires," "mental confusion; difficulty concentrating," unusual pains they never used to have before, and "headaches, pressures within the skull."[9]

Many people have gone home from these meetings to start a new life of strange experiences (that they wrongly attribute to the Holy Spirit and the working of

God in their lives) such as:

1) Heat, strange activity, and/or blissful sensations in the head, particularly in the crown area;

2) Increased creativity: new interests in self-expression and spiritual communication through music, art, poetry, etc.;

3) Ecstasy, bliss, and intervals of tremendous joy, love, peace, and compassion;

4) Spontaneous vocalizations (including laughing and weeping) [which] are as unintentional and uncontrollable as hiccoughs, hearing an inner sound or sounds, classically described as a flute, drum, waterfall, birds singing, bees buzzing but which may also sound like roaring, whooshing, or thunderous noises or like ringing in the ears."[10]

Many people have attributed these strange experiences to the Holy Spirit while all along not knowing that what they got was a kundalini awakening a) when they had someone lay hands on them or when they simply happened to be in the presence of someone "on fire" or b) as they practiced soaking prayer or other types of contemplative prayer.

Shortly after I started researching this, I came across a YouTube video where Heidi Baker was preaching. At prayer time Heidi placed her hands on a young man who started manifesting by writhing on the floor, shouting, and mourning. Heidi declared, "I think he got it,"[11] as she watched him. I can't help wondering now whether it was a kundalini awakening the young man got. Whatever it was I would not want it, and I would not want anyone I know to get it.

Many Christians will flock to conferences where these kundalini-type manifestations are happening. They are so hungry for God that they will literally run to the front to have hands laid on them or will rejoice when the preacher looks over at the section in which they are sitting and yells fire, "bam," or "more Lord," and people around go tumbling down supposedly "whacked" by the Spirit.

Many people will listen as speaker after speaker tells them stories (with occasional sprinkling of scripture verses) and tells them how they will get "undone," "unraveled," "whacked," or "drunk in the glory." All the while not knowing that if they are the unlucky ones that night, they will get a kundalini awakening and lay on the floor laughing uncontrollably, experience waves of euphoria, or a vision of an angel (which is really a demon) or any other manifestation as listed above. I say unlucky, of course, because while they will be thinking this is of God, they are just opening themselves up to demonic activity, which is what kundalini awakening is all about in reality. It is an occult practice that I believe has been ushered into the Church of Jesus Christ and many are falling victim.

One of Three Categories

If you have been in any such meetings or have had hands laid on you to receive "more," you are in one of three categories: 1) you have been having strange and often scary experiences as discussed earlier in this chapter, and you keep wondering what do to get rid of or overcome these experiences. You may never have associated them with the conferences, prayer meeting, soaking prayers, or "carpet times," but all you know is that you have been concerned and scared. If you are in this category, your best bet and only hope is to cry to God for deliverance. Repent for having opened yourself to the enemy, ask God to cleanse and restore you, and, of course, come out from among these people.

The other category 2) is you have been having

strange experiences all right, but you have all along associated some of the "positive" ones (like psychic-like abilities, being able to read people auras, extra perception, revelations, ecstasy, unusual feelings, or flow of electricity through your body, etc.) with the working of the Holy Spirit, and the negative ones (like illness, mood swings, aches, or strange dreams) with Satan who you believe is trying to attack you because of what God is doing.

The first thing is to realize that you really have been deceived. Those teachers who did this to you are wolves in sheep's clothing. They are using counterfeit miracles, signs, and wonders to deceive, and you have fallen prey. Realize that these manifestations are not of God. Repent for having opened yourself to the enemy, ask God to cleanse and restore you, and, of course, come out from among these people. Stop practicing any element of meditation, whether it be called soaking prayer, centering prayer, lectio divina or contemplative prayer. Cut ties with anything related to Bethel (Redding, California), anything related to Catch the Fire (Toronto), anything related to IHOP (out of Kansas), or anything related to the names listed in chapter 9. Mind you, these three cities (Redding,

Toronto, and Kansas) are fondly known in NAR circles as the Three Rivers, which even though they started separately eventually came together for a common goal.

The final category 3) is you could be one who has spent a lot of time in these meetings/conferences, have read books, listened to video messages, etc. You feel drawn to these leaders because they seem to know something you don't and they seem to have miracles, signs, and wonders following them, giving them an element of "authenticity." Moreover, when you consider the other churches that are not yet subscribed to this supposed move of God, they appear dead to you, are on the other extreme, and you have no desire to be associated with them because you are hungry for more of God, you want to see God, and you want to be "all out" for him. You are drawn to these people and meetings because there seems to be life, activity, and excitement, and you want your Christian life to be full of life, activity, and excitement!

What's more? These people seem to be having results. People are being healed, people are being saved, churches are growing by tens and hundreds, and new congregations are being planted. Surely, these people are bearing fruit and for that reason you have stayed with them. In addition, most of your friends and family might be the same as you. True, you have never had these manifestations; and true, at some times you may have wondered whether they are of God; and true, sometimes you may have asked God to let you experience something only if it is of him. You may have had mixed feelings at times but for other reasons, plus the fact that nobody has ever explained what is wrong with these meetings or manifestations, you have stayed.

For those in this third category, I would say the same. Now you know, and you need to cut ties. My guess is that your very hesitation and occasional prayer for God's guidance and protection is what may have kept you from plunging in (it is said that for kundalini or any other spiritual awakening, "being open to" is one of the primary requirements for "success"). Thank God for his protection and mercy and then come out from among them and be ye separate.

A Word About Christian Music

Every generation has its tastes when it comes to

music. Music that was popular in the 60s was different from the 70s, which is different from that of the 90s and of the 2000s. If you are a parent, you know that your kids have different tastes from yours, and they probably think of your type of music preference as ancient—similar to what you might have thought of your parents' taste. This same phenomenon is experienced when it comes to church/worship music. Many churches have had to deal with the debate of music preferences between the younger and older. Many churches, in an attempt to satisfy both, use a combination of hymns and contemporary Christian music (CCM), and they may find that increasingly CCM is winning.

However, many are concerned about CCM and warn about potential dangers. David Cloud, who is a musician and former New Ager, is a great example of those who are giving these warnings. He has a series of YouTube videos where he gives a great presentation on the dangers of CCM, and I highly recommend listening to his video, "foreign spirit contemporary worship music".[12] However, it is not the debate on which music to play on Sunday that I wish to comment on, but rather a far more critical element.

Among the newer forms of "worship" music that are being introduced in Christian circles are some that are downright dangerous because—you guessed it—they lead to the same problem I have mentioned all along, that of blanking the mind. Specifically, this dangerous music will appear in such names as Christian electronic dance music (EDM), Christian trance music, Christian techno dance music, Christian dubstep music, Ekstasis dance, and Christian house music, among others.

The problem with most of this music is not so much the lyrics but the roots and style. The roots of most of this music is occultic. EDM and all the others are not new styles of music, necessarily. What is new and growing is adding the word "Christian"; throwing in "Jesus," "God," and "Father" in the lyrics; and then introducing it, especially to young people. What makes it occultic is the type of beats, rhythm, and associated style of dancing, which are all geared toward producing a trance-like state in the mind of the participant. This trance-like state is the very medium that evil spirits need in order to lead participants into supernatural experiences. This music is commonly introduced to the young through youth conferences, CDs, or downloadable music.

Another category of dangerous music that gets sneaked in is binaural beats music. Simply described, this is the kind of music where the use of headphones is required because it uses the idea of each ear listening to different rhythms, beats, or frequency. The intended result is that the brainwaves would be entrained or synchronized to a different frequency from that in either ear. This brain entrainment can result in an altered state of consciousness, which once again plays into the enemy's trap. Unfortunately, some of the soaking prayer CDs available for sale or for free on the Internet are based on binaural beats.

My goal is to encourage you to not just accept everything that is presented just because it mentions Jesus, God, or the Holy Spirit. Be a wise consumer. The fact that the musician has good intentions does not mean that his or her music cannot fall into these dangerous categories. If you are a parent, take interest in what is being presented to your children in way of music. Danger lurks out there.

7

MIXING THE HOLY WITH THE PROFANE

One day I was reading Psalm 103. I was actually going through it in an attempt to memorize the entire psalm, and while working on verse 7, a thought came to my mind. The verse says, "He made known his ways unto Moses, his acts unto the children of Israel." My thought was *maybe I should read the writings of Moses with a specific goal of finding out these ways that God made known to Moses.* It seemed like a great Bible study project, and Deuteronomy seemed like an excellent place to start.

At that time I had already started to learn about the NAR and EC and the deception that is being propagated by the leaders in these movements, and I had also zeroed in on contemplative prayer as the most dangerous of all the teachings because as I said earlier, it is the pinnacle of what Satan is trying to deceive people into. Little did I know how much I would learn about the dangers of contemplative prayer from this Bible study project. I saw and understood sections of scripture in ways I had not understood them before.

Allow me to share what I learned about what God was showing Moses—the ways that God was showing to Moses. I will do this in form of a summary (in my own words). The summary spans the next several pages, but please read through it so you can appreciate the point I am making about what we can learn about the dangers of contemplative prayer from a study of what God revealed about himself to Moses.

Summary of What God Revealed to Moses (in my own words)

In Deuteronomy, God is essentially saying to Moses and the Children of Israel:

> I brought you out of Egypt in a spectacular manner because I do not want you to ever forget. I have shown you my power, and now I am going to teach you my ways.

> I brought you out of Egypt because 1) I made a promise to your ancestors Abraham, Isaac, and Jacob, 2) I chose you and I love you, and 3) I desire to give you this land as I promised. I am giving you this land a) because I chose and promised to and b) because of the evil practices of the people now dwelling in the land. Whatever you do, do not copy any of their ways because if you do, I will not be able to spare you either.

> I brought you out when my timing was completed "to the very day." (Exodus 2:41) I planned it, I timed it, and when the timing was up, I made it happen.

I brought you out by way of the desert because I wanted to bring you to my mountain where I would continue to reveal myself to you and to teach you my ways. I had no intention of taking you through the short way. I had planned and I had told Moses that I wanted him to bring you through my mountain.

However, the more I worked with you the more it became clear that you are a stubborn and stiff-necked people. You pushed my limits: you provoked me to anger over and over through your presumptuous behavior, by refusing to acknowledge what I was doing among you, by ignoring my instructions and counsel, and by testing me. You provoked me so much that I was ready to be done with you if Moses had not prayed for you.

Going forward, please know a few things about me:

1) I am a gracious and merciful God, slow to anger and plenteous in mercy.

2) I am a covenant-keeping God, which is why you are here.

3) I am a holy God. Be careful while in my presence because I am also a consuming fire.

4) I am a jealous God. Repeat. I am a jealous God. I will not tolerate other gods in any way, shape, or form. Stay away from other gods. Have nothing to do with the gods of the people who now dwell in the land you are going to possess.

5) I am slow to anger, but I do get angry when provoked. And when I do, I can be as harsh as I am kind. Do not provoke my anger.

6) It is my delight to help you, fight your battles, give you victory, make you rejoice, and provide bountifully for you. However, for me to do this, certain conditions have to be right. One, I must be your only God. Two, you must constantly purge evil from your midst. To this end I will give you my laws and teach you my ways. I will make my instructions to you very detailed and clear so that you will be able to

live in the land and never have a need to copy any of the ways of the people I am driving out from the land. My laws will cover every aspect of your lives and needs. Do not seek the ways of these people because their ways will lead you to their gods—and that is where I draw the line. Remember, I am a jealous God.

There are three main goals for the instructions and laws I am giving you:

A: The first category is so that you will know me, know how to approach me, and know how to worship me. I say it again: do not ever worship me the way these people worship their gods!

B: The second set of laws are to help you know how to live with one another and how to deal with stuff as it happens. The goal of this is so that you can constantly remember to purge any evil from your midst. If there is evil in your midst, I cannot be in your midst, so you have to constantly purge and cleanse any smudges of evil. Some of the laws in this category might appear harsh or like "overkill," but I am doing it this way to make it crystal clear 1) that it is imperative that you remove smudges of evil if I am to walk among you and 2) so that you remove such evil in such a way that the message is clear to those who remain in order to minimize the possibility of repeat.

C: The third category of instructions is so that you may know the future—how I will respond to you based on your choices. If you stay with me and walk carefully in my ways, I will establish you in the land, multiply you and bless you beyond what you can imagine. I will surround you, protect you, provide abundantly, give you peace on all sides, and let you enjoy the good of the land and all my blessings. However, if you choose the ways of these people and hence their gods, it will go for you pretty much as it has gone for them. I will uproot you from the land, the curses of your sins will follow you, and I will not be able to reach out to you. Indeed, it will be as though I am fighting against you. Please note, however, that because of my promise to Abraham, Isaac, and Jacob and my love for you, I will leave room so that if—while you are in other lands in exile (or at any time for that matter)—you repent and call upon me, I will hear and take pity on you and even restore you.

At the risk of repeating myself over and over again, please remember that I am not giving you this land because of your goodness. You are a stubborn people! I am giving you this land because of my promise and because of the sins of the people you are going to dispossess. Know for a fact that if you follow their ways, I will dispossess you of the land, too, and I will be against you and it will not be well with you.

> [I] the LORD your God will cut off before you the nations you are about to invade and dispossess. But when you have driven them out and settled in their land, and after they have been destroyed before you, be careful not to be ensnared by inquiring about their gods, saying, "How do these nations serve their gods? We will do the same." You must not worship the LORD your God in their way, because in worshiping their gods, they do all kinds of detestable things the LORD hates. They even burn their sons and daughters in the fire as sacrifices to their gods (Deuteronomy 12:29–31 NIV).

Above is my summary of what God revealed to Moses and to the children of Israel as summed up in Deuteronomy. I have chosen to end with quoting Chapter 12 verses 29–31 because it leads in to the next topic I wish to discuss still in connection to contemplative prayer.

Does Satan own anything? When the NAR and EC leaders teach on questionable practices such as out of body experiences, encounters with angels, etc.— (note that these practices are made possible when one engages in contemplative prayer), they have a way of justifying it. Basically, what they say or try to convince the readers or listeners to believe is that, yes, meditation and its associated experiences and practices are common in the New Age and in occultism, but Satan is a thief. He owns nothing. He has stolen these practices from us, and we need to reclaim them.

First of all, this is a lie: Satan does own things. And, no, he has not stolen these practices from us. They are his ideas. He owns ideas, and if you doubt this, just read the account of the Garden of Eden in Genesis. When Satan approached Eve in the form of a serpent, he brought along something that he owns—an idea. The idea worked. Satan owns ideas, he owns lies, and he owns disobedience. The notion that he is stealing something from the Christians is preposterous, or, well, it is another one of his lies!

God told the Israelites to not even enquire about the practices of these people and not to copy any of their styles of worship. Why? The reason is because the practices were demonic. I believe this applies to today and we should keep the same attitude. We are not to enquire of the practices of the New Agers or Hindu yogis, and we are not to copy any of their styles of "worship" because they are doctrines of demons. We are in the days of the end when Paul said, "The Spirit clearly says that in later times some will abandon the faith and follow deceiving spirits and things taught by demons" (1 Timothy 4:1 NIV).

You might be asking, "But who is saying to copy the practices of the New Agers?" In chapter 5, I cited Jim Goll who first suggests that "words like contemplation, meditation and centering and quietness" have a "modern association with the occult, Eastern mysticism and New Age" and then encourages the reader of his book with "do not let the enemy steal what God has ordained. Do not be afraid of these unusual ways of the Holy Spirit. . . ."[1] Goll is essentially saying that things such as astral projection, open heaven visions, are God-ordained but stolen by the enemy, and we should not let the enemy win by being afraid to enter into the practices.

Another NAR leader by the name of Jonathan Welton says that such things as "having a spirit guide, trances, meditation, auras," and so on "actually belong to the church but they have been stolen and cleverly repackaged" or counterfeited by the New Age.[2] Jonathan actually says that when you see such a New Age counterfeit, you should "take it as the Lord presenting you with an opportunity to reclaim" what once belonged to the church but has been stolen.[3]

I could give one painful example after another. The reality is that it is no secret. These teachers do not hide the fact that these practices have occult connections. They proactively come out and say that, yes, there is a connection but 1) it was stolen so let's go reclaim it, 2) if it is God-ordained, then it is okay, or 3) do not be afraid if the New Age practitioners use these methods and access the evil spirit realm, but if

Christians use these methods, they access the holy realm. It is heartbreaking to read these things from leaders who are being looked upon as role models by our young people. We need to be aware and on the lookout, if not for our own sakes, for the sake of our children.

We Are Not to Mix

Deuteronomy is full of appeals by God to his children. If you read the book again with this idea in mind, you will, like me, notice some verses that you may never have noticed before, where God is expressly warning against copying styles of worship from the people they will find in the land. Someone may say to me, "Yes, but that's the Old Testament, and their conditions were different from ours."

Have you ever thought about the fact that without the Old Testament we would know considerably less about the character of God the Father? Yes, we are not to offer the sacrifices that they offered, and, yes, there are many ways the expectations on us who know Jesus Christ as Savior are different from those on the Israelites in that time. But when it comes to the nature and character of God, he does not change. The things that made him ache for his people then would still make him ache today. The only difference is that in those days when they sinned they had to rely on the blood of animal sacrifices to cleanse their sins, while today we have the blood of the eternal covenant, that of our Lord Jesus. But I put it to you that God is the same now as he was then.

The things that happened in the Old Testament happened as examples for us so that we would not fall into the same traps they fell into or commit the same sins they committed. Paul said this very clearly:

> For I do not want you to be ignorant of the fact, brothers and sisters, that our ancestors were all under the cloud and that they all passed through the sea. They were all baptized into Moses in the cloud and in the sea. They all ate the same spiritual food and drank the same spiritual drink; for they drank from the spiritual rock that accompanied them, and that rock was Christ. Nevertheless, God was not pleased with most of them; their bodies were scattered in the wilderness. Now these things occurred as examples to keep us from setting our hearts on evil things as they did. Do not be idolaters, as some of them were; as it is written: "The people sat down to eat and drink and got up to indulge in revelry." We should not commit sexual immorality, as some of them did—and in one day twenty-three thousand of them died. We should not test Christ, as some of them did—and were

killed by snakes. And do not grumble, as some of them did—and were killed by the destroying angel. These things happened to them as examples and were written down as warnings for us, on whom the culmination of the ages has come. So, if you think you are standing firm, be careful that you don't fall! (1 Corinthians 10:1–12 NIV)

When we see a warning in the Old Testament, we do well to ponder on how it applies to us, based on the scripture passage above. In the next chapter I will continue on this same topic on how we must not copy any of what the enemy is doing.

The deceiving teachers say that we need to reclaim what the enemy has stolen and they use this argument as justification for engaging in the questionable practices.

NOTHING TO RECLAIM

When you travel on an international return flight, after you retrieve your luggage, you see two exit signs. One is labeled *Nothing to Declare*, and this is the one you take if you do not have items in your luggage that the authorities want you to declare. We who are in Christ should keep away from those who are teaching that we have something to reclaim from the enemy camp; we have nothing to reclaim. When we see God literally begging his people to keep away from other gods and not to even be curious about how they do things and then we turn around and see so-called Christian leaders teaching New Age occultist practices and justifying these teaches by saying that we are reclaiming them, we know there is something wrong. We are to stay away from such.

The theme that we should not copy from the enemy is prevalent in scripture. Another way it is taught is the idea of mixing. God wants us to learn to put a difference between the holy and the profane. Please read the following portion from Ezekiel 22: 23–28 (NIV):

> Again the word of the LORD came to me: "Son of man, say to the land, 'You are a land that has not been cleansed or rained on in the day of wrath.' There is a conspiracy of her princes within her like a roaring lion tearing its prey; they devour people, take treasures and precious things and make many widows within her. Her priests do violence to my law and profane my holy things; **they do not distinguish between the holy and the common; they teach that there is no difference between the unclean and the clean;** and they shut their eyes to the keeping of my Sabbaths, so that I am profaned among them. Her officials within her are like wolves tearing their prey; they shed blood and kill people to make unjust gain. **Her prophets whitewash these deeds for them by false visions**

and lying divinations. They say, 'This is what the Sovereign LORD says'—when the LORD has not spoken." *(emphasis mine)*

This scripture portion is loaded. The first part of verse 26 in the KJV Bible says, "Her priests have violated my law, and **have profaned mine holy things: they have put no difference between the holy and profane, neither have they shewed difference between the unclean and the clean**." The key ideas jumping out of these verses for me are that of not putting a difference between the holy and profane and that of prophets issuing false visions and divinations to justify the wrong acts (verse 28).

Anything coming from Satan, regardless of where he got it from, is profane and unclean. We are to distinguish and never rationalize mixing it with what is from God. Suggesting in their teachings that practices—such as astral projection, contemplative prayer, open heaven visions and so on—somehow belonged to us, were stolen, and we should therefore reclaim them sounds eerily similar to mixing the holy with profane.

Again in Ezekiel 44:23 God was addressing through Ezekiel the duties and responsibilities of the priests when he said, "And they shall teach my people the difference between the holy and profane, and cause them to discern between the unclean and the clean." It is important to God that we learn the difference between the holy and profane and that we keep away from mixing the two at any time for any reason. In contrast, the NAR and EC leaders are essentially teaching people to mix the holy and profane.

As I continued to explore the use of the word profane, I saw another striking verse: Ezekiel 28:16. First note that Ezekiel 28 is popularly believed to be referencing how Satan became Satan. In verse 16 God is therefore saying to Satan, "By the multitude of thy merchandise they have filled the midst of thee with violence, and thou hast sinned: **therefore I will cast thee as profane out of the mountain of God:** and I will destroy thee, O covering cherub, from the midst of the stones of fire." *(emphasis mine)*

Satan was cast out of heaven as profane. His ways are profane. We are not to mix them in any way, shape, or form with the things of God. We are to turn away from the profane, abstain from its appearance, and flee from it. Holy, we are to pursue. We are to sanctify God in our hearts and lives, and we must never mix anything that even has the appearance of profane with any aspects of our lives—no matter how sugar-coated it is and no matter what promise it offers.

One of the reasons the NAR movement has acquired such a large following and acceptance among evangelical Christians today (and make no mistake about it the movement is growing like a wildfire on a windy day) is that they claim to have miracles accompanying their teachings. Indeed, another name for the NAR is the miracles and wonders movement.

The saying *all that glitters is not gold* comes to mind. All that claims to be of God is not necessarily of God. Just because it is a miracle, sign, or a wonder does not mean that it is of God. Do not be persuaded to follow or subscribe to the teachings of any teacher just because he or she has what appears to be miracles, signs, and wonders. For one, Satan has his own miracles, signs, and wonders. The Bible calls them "signs and lying wonders" (2 Thessalonians 2:9) or "counterfeit miracles, signs, and wonders" (NIV). My point here is as follows: it may be a miracle, a sign, or a wonder, but beware because that does not mean it is of God. Be not deceived.

This leads to a good question: How then can one quickly tell which sign and wonder is not of God? For one, I think before we submit ourselves to anyone's teaching, we owe it to ourselves to find out what this person is all about. How do they treat the Word of God? Are they asking you to do something that is not supported by scripture (like contemplative prayer, for example)? That said, God gave his children a very interesting way of deciphering who is a true prophet and how to tell true signs and wonders from the counterfeit.

> If a prophet, or one who foretells by dreams, appears among you and **announces to you a sign or wonder, and if the sign or wonder spoken of takes place, and the prophet says, "Let us follow other gods" (gods you have not known) "and let us worship them," you must not listen to the words of that prophet or dreamer. The LORD your God is testing you to find out whether you love him with all your heart and with all your soul** (Deuteronomy 3:1–3 *emphasis mine)*

In the NAR for example, there are also many who claim to be prophets or dreamers of dreams. The teaching in the passage above is: do not assess, follow, or otherwise endorse anyone's teaching simply because something he or she pronounced came to pass. The rest of Deuteronomy 13 continues to offer stern warnings against following anyone's suggestions if these suggestions are pointing you to other gods you have not known. Everything God wants us to know and follow is in his written Word. He has no need to provide new revelations as these false teachers are claiming.

Let me say again: just because it is a miracle, a sign, or a wonder does not mean it is of God, and it does not give you a blanket license to follow the teachings of such a person—especially if the teachings are leading you to follow other gods that you do not know. New Age based teachings, such as contemplative prayer, are a classic example of teachings from other gods. Beware and stay away from these false dreamers and false prophets.

I know I have quoted heavily from the book of Deuteronomy in making the case that we are not to borrow from New Age-type teachings. Please read Deuteronomy and ask yourself whether I am making a fair case, and I hope you will find it so. After I finished studying Deuteronomy, I continued on with the theme of finding out how God made known his way to Moses as stated in Psalm 103:7 which I cited earlier. So I read through the books written by Moses—Exodus, Leviticus, and Numbers—and I was amazed how the same theme of *have nothing to do with the practices of people who follow other gods* keeps coming up. God instructed in very clear terms that his people were not to borrow, copy, or in any way associate with the practices of the people whose land he was giving them to possess. Today, many in the NAR seem to take it lightly when they are talking about some of their practices, which have connections to the Occult/New Age as I previously mentioned.

Do Not Desire the Gold

When God gave his people the Promised Land, they were to destroy everything that pointed to other gods. When they came across graven images, they were not to take the gold or silver that is on the images!

> The graven images of their gods shall ye burn with fire: thou shalt not desire the silver or gold that is on them, nor take it unto thee, lest thou be snared therein: for it is an abomination to the LORD thy God (Deuteronomy 7:25).

Think about it; the gold and the silver are metals. Surely you can extract them and even purify them because they are just metals, right? But God said not to desire these otherwise precious metals or take them or else they will be a snare unto them.

From the above passage in Deuteronomy 7, it is fair to conclude that anything that is associated with evil (e.g., the precious metals on the graven images) we are not to desire or take to ourselves in any way. Not only is it plain, wrong, and disobedient to do so, it will be a snare. God called these practices an abomination to him. We should have the same attitude; we are not to desire anything associated with New Age or occult practices, not matter how gold-like it appears to be. It is wrong, disobedient, and it will be a snare to those who desire and take such to themselves.

Do Not Marry Them

In Deuteronomy 7, God made it very clear that his people were not to intermarry with the people they were going to dispossess. In verses 3 and 4 he gave the reason:

> Neither shalt thou make marriages with them; thy daughter thou shalt not give unto his son, nor his daughter shalt thou take unto thy son. **For they will turn away thy son from following me, that they may serve other gods: so will the anger of the LORD be kindled against you, and destroy thee suddenly**. *(emphasis mine)*

Any association with these people that they were going to dispossess would cause the children of God to turn away and serve other gods, and this would lead to kindling God's anger. God was very serious about this topic. He said: do not make any covenant with them (verse 2), do not serve their gods for they will be a snare to thee (verse 16), and destroy all their places of worship, completely.

Do Not Import Worship Ideas

God does not want to be served or worshiped with borrowed ideas. There is more than enough instructions in his Word on how he wants to be served and worshipped (complete with songs—I mean psalms, I might add). He did not want his children to borrow worship ideas from the Canaanites.

On the topic of borrowed ideas, a good example exists from the book of Jeremiah. Now, just a bit of recap: what happened is that after they possessed and settled in the land, the Israelites did exactly what God warned and begged them not to do throughout the writings of Moses. Do you remember when God told them in Deuteronomy 12:4, **"You must not worship the LORD your God in their way,"** meaning please do not worship me the way these people worship their gods? Well, the Israelites did that. They enquired after the practices of other gods, they went after these gods, and they did exactly what God had told them not to do. In the book of Jeremiah, God is again begging them to stop, repent, and turn away from these practices. They would not. Eventually they went to exile just like God had told them would happen.

In Jeremiah 6, God is confronting the people through the Prophet Jeremiah. Of particular interest, God mentions that they worship him with imported incense: "To what purpose cometh there to me incense from Sheba, and the sweet cane from a far country? Your burnt offerings are not acceptable, nor your sacrifices sweet unto me" (Jeremiah 6:20).

The Israelites in Jeremiah's day went ahead and imported incense from Sheba, offered it to God, and God was furious about it! In an earlier verse in the same chapter in Jeremiah, God was telling the people: "Thus saith the LORD, Stand ye in the ways, and see, and ask for the old paths, where is the good way, and walk therein, and ye shall find rest for your souls. But they said, We will not walk therein" (Jeremiah 6:16). I interpret this to mean that God is asking them to stay with the old paths, the good way that he has revealed, and walk in it in order to find rest for their souls and instead of going to new ways and importing ideas which were an abomination to him.

It is worth noting, in relation to the verses about incense from Sheba, that in the Bible the offering of incense was an Old Testament form of worship, and I believe for Christians the laws about incense points to and teaches us about prayer (Psalms 141:2, Luke 1:10, Revelation 5:8, and 8:3–4). We are not to burn incense—it is not a New Testament teaching, but references to burning of incense translate to a picture of prayer for us. That is what I believe, but please check the biblical references I have provided to see if you agree before you engage my argument below.

The instructions about incense were clear as given in Exodus 30. Among the instructions was that it was only to be offered by priests under very specific conditions with no deviation from the specific rules and also that no incense was to be burnt at home. The laws about offering incense were clearly not to be messed around with. Indeed, on their first day on the job, two priests (Nadab and Abihu, in Leviticus chapter 10) took these laws lightly and offered what the Bible calls strange fire before God, and they died instantly. The message was clear: when it came to incense, do it the right way, follow the prescriptions, and do not deviate.

Is it fair to suggest that this is teaching us that when it comes to prayer, we should pray according to what is clearly taught in God's Word and that we should not bring in strange or imported ideas? I think so, and I go as far as to suggest to you that contemplative prayer is an example of offering strange incense. Do not offer to God this strange incense because he is not interested in it.

Nadab and Abihu offered strange incense before God, and God was furious. The Israelites in the time of Jeremiah offered imported incense (instead of using the recipe and laws God had given about incense) before God, and he saw it as an abomination. Contemplative prayer and all related practices are imported, figuratively and literally. Literally in the sense that they really do come from Eastern religions such as Buddhism and Hinduism, and figuratively in that they are foreign to the Bible and hence they are imported.

I have tried to show how the argument that we should reclaim New Age-type practices and use them to access the supernatural is wrong and unbiblical. Please check out the scriptures I have cited to make my case and decide whether it is a fair case. I really do not want to you to take my word for it. Taking people's word for it is what is getting so many people into deception.

I have also tried to show that contemplative prayer is foreign to the Bible and is an example of the type of practices that God is very clear we must stay away from. Contemplative prayer is not prayer. Calling it prayer is another deceptive gimmick of the enemy. Just because they call it prayer does not make it prayer. What would make it prayer is if it is taught in the Bible, and it is not.

One way to learn about biblical prayer would be to look at individuals in the Bible who prayed. How did they pray? Do any of them empty their minds so that they can hear God? The answer would be no. Indeed when we look at people whose prayers are recorded, such as Moses, Nehemiah, Ezra, and David, we will find that their prayers are not absentminded-type activity. One of the most commonly used words with respect to people approaching God to talk to him (aka pray) is beseech. Moses used the word beseech often (I can count approximately six times in my Bible) as did David and Nehemiah. Beseeching is a very active process. I will look in-depth at this word and what it entails in chapter 11.

When Jesus taught his disciples to pray, one of the first things he warned them about, even before he taught them how to pray (what we call the Lord's Prayer), was to avoid vain repetitions like the heathen do (Matthew 6:7). Please note that some forms of contemplative prayer require you to take a word or a phrase and repeat it over and over and over, and this is actually what helps empty the mind. When you pray, you talk to God, and talking requires an active and engaged mind.

In chapter 11 I will share some thoughts about prayer as taught in the Bible. I have spent so much time in this book describing a wrong type of prayer, so it is only fair that I say something about the right kind of prayer as taught directly in the Bible.

But before I talk about prayer, I now would like to point to names of leaders who teach contemplative prayer and related practices.

9

LEADERS, SPEAKERS, AND AUTHORS TO AVOID

I have read quite a few books authored by individuals from the NAR or EC, and one notable key is the way each author will point readers to others in the camp either by quoting them repeatedly or by suggesting you should read this and that book. I am not saying this is a bad thing in and of itself because it is normal. After all, I am about to recommend books and resources that you would refer to if you wanted to learn more about the NAR or EC. What I mean to say is that it is easy to follow the trail of who is teaching what or who is endorsing what by keeping an eye on whom recommends whom.

The website www.lighthousetrailsresearch.com/blog/?p=9707 lists *Top 50 "Christian" Contemplative Books – A "NOT RECOMMENDED Reading List" and 25 Christian "Bridgers" to Them*. This list of fifty books includes well known, influential authors such as Tony Campolo, Rick Warren, Tony Jones, Brian Maclaren, Mark Yaconelli, David Spangler, Richard Foster, Larry Crabb, Brennan Manning, Henri Nouwen, and Alan Jones, among others

The list of twenty-five Christian Bridgers or the leaders who embrace, emulate, or promote the works of the fifty authors include people such as Mark Driscoll, Eugene Peterson, Shane Claiborne, Dallas Willard, Dan Kimball, Beth Moore, Philip Yancey, Rob Bell, Doug Pagitt, Leonard Sweet, Donald Miller, and Bill Hybels, among others.

The website www.lighthousetrailsresearch.com/blog/?p=8359 provides a list of a hundred "top contemplative proponents evangelical Christian turn to today." The list contains names of individuals who actively teach contemplative spirituality and includes the above names plus others such as Jim Goll, John Ortberg, Mark Virkler, Max Lucado, Ruth Harley Barton, Todd Bentley, and Tony Jones, among others.

Another website www.zedekiahlist.com/ has a list of over 700 well-known Christian speakers who have publicly said something unscriptural. For each name, the site provides the actual quotations of the unscriptural things said. Most of the names I have listed below and those on the websites above are also listed on the Zedekiah list.

Another website that provides names of these leaders is https://simplicityinchrist.wordpress.com/list-of-pretendersteachers/. This website provides what it calls a list of pretenders or "teachers, promoters, advocates, supporters, proponents, and defenders of Spiritual Formation (metaphysics, contemplative spirituality, spiritual disciplines [silence, solitude, stillness, lectio divina, centering, breath, listening, soaking prayer]) who ignore the power of the Gospel of Jesus Christ and subscribe to a 'new' spirituality." For each name, the website provides quotes and links to materials related to the person.

From the lists and names available on the three

websites provided above, I hope that you, the reader, can get a sense of the people that are knowing or unknowing deceivers. I should note here that I have not encountered each and every one of the individuals listed in the websites provided above; however, I can say that from my own research leading up to this book, I have engaged materials, whether in print or audio form, from the people listed below, and it is based on this engagement that I have put together my thoughts in this book.

1) Those associated directly or indirectly with the NAR such as: C. Peter Wagner, Chuck Pierce, Bill Johnson, Rick Joyner, Jim Goll, Todd Bentley, John & Carol Arnott, Randy Clark, Patricia King, Heidi Baker, Cindy Jacobs, Stacy Campbell, Mahesh Chavdah, Mike Bickle, Paul Cain, Bob Jones, Jill Austin, Paul Jackson, Sid Roth, Bill Hamon, Katie Souza, Sharnel Woverton, Kris Vallotton, Jason Westerfield, Joshua Mills, Kobus Van Rensburg, Lance Wallnau, Lou Engle, Matt Sorger, Georgian Banov & Winnie Banov, Jonathan Welton, Shawn Bolz, and John Crowder, among others.

2) Those associated directly or indirectly with the Emergent Church Movement such as: Brian McLaren, Rob Bell, Rick Warren, Peter Rollins, Tony Jones, Tony Campolo, Doug

Pagitt, Shane Claiborne, and William Paul Young, among others.

3) Others (who may be associated with the NAR, EC, or other movements like Word of Faith) such as: Benny Hinn, Kenneth and Gloria Copeland, Yonggi Cho, and Rodney-Howard Browne, among others.

In addition, on my own website[1] I have provided a site with links to many resources (mainly YouTube-based) where many of the people I have mentioned are teaching or otherwise sharing their ideas. I also provide a list of useful resources that you can explore if you desire to conduct more research on these matters.

As I indicated earlier, the only reason behind naming names is that interested readers would be able to know exactly what kind of teachings to stay away from, and since the teachings are being propagated by people, naming the individuals is not avoidable. More than naming/knowing people, however, what is important is to know what is wrong about certain teachings. In this book I have tried to point to what is wrong with any teaching that leads one to empty the mind. I have specifically focused on contemplative prayer, which is also taught under other names such as soaking prayer, centering prayer, lectio divina, silent prayer, and breath prayers. I take no pleasure in naming individuals, but I would not achieve the goal of helping people stay away from these teachings if I do not, for example, take Jim Goll's writings and show how they are deceptive as I did in chapter 5. My naming of individuals is not a statement of whether they are genuine Christians or not. As I have said repeatedly, many of them may be doing what they are doing unknowingly, and I would hope that they will realize and turn.

Too Much Trouble?

One of the saddest times in the history of Israel is when one of the Kings (Jeroboam) decided that it was too much trouble to the people in the northern part of Israel to travel to the Temple of God at Jerusalem—the place God had selected as the place to offer sacrifices to him, so he set up golden calves, shrines, and altars; appointed priests of his own choosing; changed the special days that God had instituted; and told and encouraged the people to follow his example (see 1 Kings 12: 28-33).

I was motivated to write this book to highlight for you, the reader, the dangers of the false teachings that are spreading quickly and that threaten to bring about the falling away of many. I submit to you that what these leaders are doing (whether knowingly or unknowingly) is very similar to what Jeroboam did. They appear to have essentially decided that it is too much trouble to live by faith (an assurance of things hoped for), which is what we have been called to, and instead they would rather pursue experiences. In pursuit of these experiences, they have fallen into a trap of Satan and are now knowingly or unknowingly doing his bidding. Their teachings are taking many away from the simplicity of the gospel and putting them in pursuit of experiences which unfortunately and sadly are leading many to another Jesus, another spirit, and another gospel.

Many of the people who are being deceived have no idea, which means this deception is working. This reminds me of a true story my sister told me not long ago.

A lady (a friend of my mom) went to the morgue hoping to catch a ride with someone in the funeral procession to the funeral of a friend. She arrived a tad early and found a group of people just heading out. As luck would have it, someone announced that there was a bus that had space for anyone who needed a ride. She hopped in and was transported to some funeral. Meanwhile, her children who were hoping to find their mother at the funeral she was supposed to be in were concerned when they could not find her, so they called her cell phone. It is only then that the lady realized she was at the wrong funeral. It is also the day her children realized she was having cognitive issues (developing Alzheimer's), but this is a true story that I share because it captures what is happening to many Christians. They have hopped into the wrong bus and while everything looks okay so far, they are being shipped to a different place than where they ought to be without any idea as of yet.

If you or anyone you know is subscribing to the teachings or ministry that is under the leadership of any of the leaders mentioned in this chapter, if you have been told that contemplative prayer in its various forms whether it be centering prayer, silent prayer, or soaking is the way to get intimacy with God, to hear God's voice, or to dwell in the secret place, you may be in danger of hopping on the wrong bus, or you may be in the wrong bus already. I am not saying you are not going to heaven—I am just saying that you are in danger of the type of deception that Satan is orchestrating, and you need to get out of these movements or their influences. The Bible says, "Wherefore come out from among them, and **be ye separate**, saith the Lord, and touch not the unclean thing; and I will receive you." (2

Corinthians 6:17 *emphasis mine*). I hope you will heed this warning.

So what do you do if you come out? Where do you even go? These people, and their teachings are everywhere. I share some thoughts in the next chapter.

10

HUNGER HIJACKED

The majority of people who have fallen prey to these false teachings are dear brothers and sisters who will tell you they are hungry for God and thirsty for more in their Christian walk, and this, in and of itself, is a good thing. However, this feeling of hunger and thirst is further deepened when you meet someone who claims to have been "there" and can teach you how to go there. You are hungry to experience more of the Holy Spirit, and then you meet someone who seems to have "figured out" the Holy Spirit and has regular like one-on-one conversations with the Holy Spirit. When this person speaks, you will listen. When they offer you how-to advice, you will listen and most likely will try. When this or another person relate to you how they visited heaven, or you watch them on Sid Roth's YouTube videos—where these heavenly visitations are dramatized for your viewing pleasure, then your hunger only gets sharpened. And when they offer a CD that will teach you how to go to *the secret place* or *have intimacy with the Father*, you will likely buy it or seek out similar resources.

What am I driving at? Your hunger for God has been or is being hijacked. First, it is being made deeper by being presented with scenarios where people like you seem to have achieved your goal or seem to know how to achieve it, and this is a hook they are luring you with to the wrong place. When you get to this wrong place, you will have real experiences, but they will not be of God. They will be counterfeits, and you will end up in one of three categories I discussed in chapter 6.

What to do then? We need to come to terms with a harsh reality and make a choice. We need to do the

---

following:

1) Search in the right place. Search for God in the pages of his Word instead of from experiences that others claim to have had. There is so much that God has revealed about himself in his Word, and you have not covered it all. Until you do, until you have combed the scriptures for all the ways God wants you to know him, then keep studying and requesting God to let you see these things that he has already revealed. *If you desire and thirst for experiences just because other people claim to have had them, you will put yourself on a path where deception can happen, and you won't know.*

2) **Faith not experiences.** Realize that we have been called to a life of faith not of experiences. When we pray, we know that God has heard, not because we have seen or have experienced something but because we have faith in him. Do not wait for a tingle, a shake, a tear, a wave of electricity, or an audible voice to confirm that God has answered. Come to God in humility, forgive those who have wronged you, thank God for all his mercy, love and goodness, and then make your requests known to him, beseeching him, calling on him, asking him with persistence, earnestness, and fervency, trusting that the

Holy Spirit is helping you—not because you feel so but because the Bible says He helps you. And then rest in your faith in God and trust him to act in his time and good pleasure. *If you learn to rely on tangible, palpable proof as evidence of effective prayer, then you are really learning to walk by sight instead of faith and will put yourself on a path where deception can happen, and you may not know it.*

3) **No one is immune.** Realize that the Bible calls the last days perilous (2 Timothy 3:1). The days we are living in may very well be these last and perilous times, and perilous means dangerous. There is danger and deception out there, and no one is immune.

4) **Deceiving spirits.** Realize that "The Spirit clearly says that in later times some will abandon the faith and follow deceiving spirits and things taught by demons. Such teachings come through hypocritical liars, whose consciences have been seared as with a hot iron" (1 Timothy 4:1–2 NIV). This means that some people will indeed abandon the faith. Have these teachers abandoned the faith? Are they following deceiving spirits and things taught by demons? Are they genuine, or are they hypocritical liars? If you are not 100 percent sure about

them, then cut ties with them. You are safer staying away from them. *If you keep following them and pursing their ideas, you are in danger of abandoning the faith, too.*

5) **Your responsibility.** Jesus said to watch that no one deceives you. You need to watch that no one deceives you. It is up to you to watch out—Jesus entrusted this responsibility to you.

6) **The Word or the Holy Spirit?** You will notice that these people really love the Holy Spirit—and do not get me wrong—it is okay to love the Holy Spirit, after all he has been given to us as our helper. But these people elevate the Holy Spirit above the Word of God. I believe one of the reasons for this is because the Holy Spirit, as they conceptualize him, is easier to work with. See, the Word is there, it is written, and everyone has access to the same Word. And even though it is possible to pull a verse out of context and use it to make a case, it is harder to do so because someone else might come and rebut the point being made by looking not only at the context but by comparing scripture with scripture. But when it comes to the Holy Spirit, it is so easy to decide for him, and no one is any the wiser as there is no real way of validating what the Holy Spirit is reported to have said to a person.

The same case applies to dreams and revelations that people claim to have had: it is impossible to validate what they reportedly saw or heard. If you have been conditioned to trusting a certain leader as an apostle or a prophet, then it is easy to simply take their word for it when it comes to the supernatural encounters they claim to have had and the messages they claim to have received from God, Jesus, or angels during these encounters.

So, what I am driving at? Reduce your reliance or trust on any message that was received by anyone who had a dream or a visitation by an "angel" or "Jesus," or from heaven in their last visit, or by the "Holy Spirit" as they were soaking, etc. *If you depend on these things, you are putting yourself on the path of deception.* Do not be consumed with seeking "a word" from anyone; do not be consumed with going around wishing someone could give you a message that they received from the Lord for you; do not go around desiring or looking for someone to prophesy over you. Yes, the Lord is more than able and more than willing to use someone to minister to you in this way but let him do it in his timing.

7) **Ask yourself.** What happens in your church, in that conference, or in that prayer meeting? Is there actual

teaching of the Word for God. Is the preaching based on a genuine interpretation of the Word? Is the goal of teaching or preaching so you can know God from the Word and apply the Word to your life, or is the Word used to justify a new idea or practice that the preacher wants to get you to try?

Is the preaching mainly stories of what happened in this meeting or that experience (with an occasional mention of a scripture that you are not even encouraged to open and read)? Is the Holy Spirit being elevated above the Word of God? Are things being done because the Holy Spirit said so, and no effort is made to show how the Word clearly says so? Are practices based primarily on a dream, a vision, or a message received by an apostle or prophet in one of his or her supernatural encounters? Are there practices that would make a visiting nonbeliever squirm or think you guys are crazy? Is the overall atmosphere honoring to the holiness of God? Is everything being done *decently and in order* (1 Corinthians 14:40), or is there more chaos than order? Is it an anything-goes kind of environment? Are there times when you have wondered whether something is okay or of God, but with time you convinced yourself that it must be?

Are there practices, miracles, or testimonies that made you uncomfortable or squirmy, but you figured maybe it's you who needs to catch up to things and therefore you rationalized that these things must be okay? Are there times you have desired an experience just because buddy so-and-so experienced it or leader so-and-so says it is okay even though you are not really sure that it is supported by scripture? Are you encouraged to check things against scripture either as the preacher speaks or after, or are you encouraged, directly or indirectly, to take his/her word for it? Is there an encouragement to take up a new practice, such as to practice more silent or soaking prayers using such-and-such a CD, read certain books, accept people of other faiths just as they are and just love them instead of evangelizing them, practice praying for people to receive miracles even though they are not believers yet, and hope that the miracles will cause them to believe?

I am not here to tell you where to go or not to go. My goal is to warn about practices that can put you on a dangerous spiritual path, and to encourage you to be aware and beware. I offer the following suggestions in summary:

Some Specific Suggestions

1) Avoid any gathering where blanking out your mind is

encouraged or taught in any shape or form—whether it be by chanting, singing repetitively, drumming, visualization, meditation, or breathing techniques.

2) Avoid any gathering where meditation-type praying is endorsed, taught, and or encouraged. This could be called soaking, silent prayer, contemplative prayer, lectio divina, prayer of the heart, or breath prayer.

3) Avoid any gathering where special laying on of hands for the purpose of "impartation" of "anointing" is practiced—if this impartation often leads to being "slain in the spirit"; having "carpet time"; being "drunk in the spirit"; being "whacked," "undone," or "unlaced"; "basking in the glory"; or going into some kind of a trance.

4) Avoid gatherings where the focus is on supernatural manifestations—whether it is gold dust or feathers, angelic orbs (whatever those are), clouds of glory, open portals, Jacob's ladder, angels appearing, out-of-body experiences, or special revelations such as dreams or visions.

5) Avoid any books or audio materials that teach the practices mentioned above. Avoid books or materials that promise that you can activate your supernatural realm-access abilities or spiritual senses.

6) Get into the Word of God. Search for God in the pages of his Word. Elevate his Word above all else. Why? The reason is because he, too, has elevated it. David said, "I will worship toward thy holy temple, and praise thy name for thy lovingkindness and for thy truth: for **thou hast magnified thy word above all thy name**" (Psalm 138:2). *(emphasis mine)*

7) Be content. By this I do not mean stop thirsting or hungering for a stronger relationship with God. However, these false teachers want to lure you to a flashy, exotic experience-based walk. But God has not called you for flashy or exotic, and he has not called you for an experience-based walk. What he is after is holiness and dependence on him **by faith.**

8) Consider the following verses (you can read them also in another Bible version if you like). All three sections come from Paul in his second letter to the Corinthians. Would these warnings apply to us today in light of the need to be aware of what's going on and watchful so that we are not deceived or lead astray?

> But I am afraid that just as Eve was deceived by the serpent's cunning, your minds may somehow be led astray from your sincere and pure devotion to Christ. For if someone comes to you and preaches a Jesus other than

Deception in the Church

the Jesus we preached, or if you receive a different spirit from the Spirit you received, or a different gospel from the one you accepted, you put up with it easily enough (2 Corinthians 11:3–4 NIV).

Be ye not unequally yoked together with unbelievers: for what fellowship hath righteousness with unrighteousness? And what communion hath light with darkness? And what concord hath Christ with Belial? Or what part hath he that believeth with an infidel? And what agreement hath the temple of God with idols? For ye are the temple of the living God; as God hath said, I will dwell in them, and walk in them; and I will be their God, and they shall be my people. Wherefore come out from among them, and be ye separate, saith the Lord, and touch not the unclean thing; and I will receive you. And will be a Father unto you, and ye shall be my sons and daughters, saith the Lord Almighty (2 Corinthians 6:14–18).

For such are false apostles, deceitful workers, transforming themselves into the apostles of Christ. And no marvel; for Satan himself is transformed into an angel of light. Therefore it is no great thing if his ministers also be transformed as the ministers of righteousness; whose end shall be according to their works (2 Corinthians 11:13–15).

How Much Poison is Enough?

Finally, there is a common saying that rat poison is typically 99 percent good stuff like cheese and only 1 percent poison. I guess the poison makers figure, 1) it might be too expensive to use 100 percent poison material,

2) why bother if 1 percent will do the job?, and 3) if it has too much poison material, the rats might be able to tell from afar and might never nibble on it. I use this idea to suggest that it is also possible to encounter this principle when it comes to deception. If any material—whether a song, a message, a book, or a video presentation—is so blatant or has *deception written all over it*, it might not do the job because the intended victims might be able to tell from afar. As well, why bother if just a little deception poison will do the job? My point is as follows: just because it does not smell like poison does not mean it cannot be poison. So if you sense or suspect even a little poison, the wise thing is to stay clear. You do not need 100 percent proof that it is poison before you keep away. If you are dealing with a ministry that has been tainted with the teachings that I (and others) are suggesting to avoid, then the wise thing to do is to stay clear. Meanwhile, launch an investigation of your own, and together we can help others stay away from poison.

11

THE EFFECTUAL FERVENT PRAYER

hat is prayer? A good study of what the Bible teaches about prayer reveals that in prayer we come to God by faith with an attitude of humility, contrition (i.e., repentance), and forgiveness. We begin by thanking and praising God for who he is and all he has done. With our mouths/lips/tongue we offer praise and adoration and express our love and gratitude to him. We do all this in the name of our Lord Jesus Christ. We then proceed to make our requests known to God. In doing so, we beseech him, we present our petitions, we entreat him, and we implore, plead, ask, request, call, supplicate, and appeal to him. This is what the people who prayed in the Bible did. What's more? We are to do these things with an attitude of belief, trust, and expectation. We are also to exercise earnestness, fervency, importunity, and persistence. We are to trust that the Holy Spirit is helping us in all this—not because we see him or feel something but because the Bible says that he helps us.

One biblical character whose prayer activity is recorded was Elijah. James reminds us that Elijah was a man just like us, and when he prayed, he saw results. Since this is what we desire—to pray effectual prayers, I believe we could learn much from how Elijah prayed. The NAR and EC leaders present contemplative prayer as a way to have powerful impactful prayer, but the Bible points us to Elijah's example as the way to pray impactful prayers. What do we know about Elijah's prayer? Let's look at the context in the book of James:

> Therefore confess your sins to each other and pray for each other so that you may be healed. The prayer of a righteous person is powerful and effective. Elijah was a

human being, even as we are. He prayed earnestly that it would not rain, and it did not rain on the land for three and a half years. Again he prayed, and the heavens gave rain, and the earth produced its crops (James 5:16–18 NIV).

In the KJV, the last part of verse says, "The effectual fervent prayer of a righteous man availeth much." Do you want to pray a prayer that is powerful and effective? Then you ought to pray like Elijah. That is what the Bible implies.

I wanted to get to the bottom of this, so I did an in-depth study of this statement from James on Elijah's prayer. I started by checking the meaning of words used in the passage. Specifically, I checked out the words: effectual, fervent, earnest, avails, and effective:[1]

- **Effectual**: producing or able to produce a desired effect
- **Avail**: effective use in the achievement of a goal
- **Earnest**: Serious in intention, purpose, or effort; showing depth and sincerity of feeling; implies having a purpose and being steadily and soberly eager in pursuing it
- **Fervent**: having or displaying a passionate intensity

If we put together these definitions, the effectual fervent prayer of a righteous man availeth much can also be said as follows: the prayer that is able to produce a desired effect, prayed with passionate intensity, is effective in the achievement of its goals.

Elijah was just like us. He had a purpose, and he prayed earnestly— meaning he steadily, eagerly, seriously, and passionately talked to God about it. This is the effectual fervent prayer that Elijah prayed. We can learn much from it. One thing that is for sure is that it was not contemplative prayer. We do not see him emptying his mind or repeating a mantra. Moses, David, and Nehemiah also prayed powerful and effective prayers. We do not see them passively sitting on a chair and trying to empty their minds by repeating a phrase. Instead, we see them engaging God.

As I mentioned above, one of the most common words used in referring to the prayers of these men is that they besought God. Other words used in reference to prayer include to supplicate, request, ask, petition, call, plead, appeal, and so on. We can learn more about what biblical prayer entails by exploring the meaning of these words:[2]

1) To beseech: to ask (someone) urgently and fervently to do something; implore; entreat. The synonyms of beseech are:

> **a) im·plore**: to beg (someone) earnestly or desperately to do something
> **b) beg**: to ask (someone) earnestly or humbly for something
> **c) en·treat**: to ask someone earnestly or anxiously

intently to do something

d) im·por·tune: to ask (someone) pressingly and persistently for or to do something

e) sup·pli·cate: to ask or beg for something earnestly or humbly

2) Ask: request (someone) to do or give something

3) Request: politely or formally ask for

4) Petition: make or present a formal request to (an authority) with respect to a particular cause

5) Call: cry out to (someone) in order to summon them or attract their attention

6) Plead: make an emotional appeal. To appeal earnestly or humbly

7) Appeal: make a serious or urgent request

8) Prayer: a solemn request for help or expression of thanks addressed to God

Prayer in the Bible involves asking, requesting, and crying out with an attitude of humility, with passionate intensity, and by persistently pursuing the matter until God makes a way. Please note that this is not to imply that God needs to be begged to do something—as though he is not willing. It is to imply that prayer is not a drive-through type of business, neither is it a passive *sit still, banish all thoughts while repeating this word or phrase* activity. It is active engagement. It involves at times making your case before God like Abraham did when he prayed for Sodom and Gomorrah. It involves opening your mouth and asking like Jesus taught in Mathew 7:7 or requesting as Paul taught in Philippians 4:6. It involves crying to God like Jesus, "Who in the days of his flesh, when he had offered up **prayers and supplications with strong crying and tears** unto him that was able to save him from death, and was heard in that he feared" (Hebrews 5:7). *(emphasis mine)*

Do not be deceived. Contemplative prayer, centering prayer, lectio divina, soaking prayer—all these are forms of mind-blanking meditation. They are not prayer, and you do not need to practice them for any reason.

12

DECEPTION: A BIBLE STUDY

My heart is heavy at the thought that we live in a world where a lot of deception has crept in and many followers of Christ are vulnerable. In this chapter I am presenting a Bible study that I conducted on the topic of deception. I did it to give myself an understanding of what the Bible says about the topic. As I indicated earlier, in order to understand any one topic, we need to gather many verses (all if possible), go through them, and consider what they are altogether saying. These days it is easy to do this because with an online Bible, for example, it is possible to type a word or phrase and gather all the verses in one document and then start going through them. That is what I did here.

In the study below, therefore, I start with a dictionary definition of deception; then I summarize what the verses are saying under six subheadings: 1) The who and what, 2) What are the most common warnings in the Bible about deception? 3) What are the main techniques used to deceive people? 4) What are the chief goals of deception? 6) What is the most important thing to remember about deception? Then I end with a table in which I summarize the techniques for deception and offer what we need to remember as we encounter various teachers and preachers.

WHAT IS THE DEFINITION OF DECEPTION?

Deceive: To cause to believe what is not true.
Involves the deliberate misrepresentation of the truth:

What are some synonyms for deception?
Synonyms: mislead, beguile, delude, dupe, hoodwink, and bamboozle. These verbs mean to lead another into

error, danger, or a disadvantageous position by underhanded means

Mislead: to lead in the wrong direction or into error of thought or action

Beguile: deceiving by means of charm or allure

To delude: to mislead the mind or judgment

Dupe: playing upon another's susceptibilities or naiveté

Hoodwink: to delude by trickery

Bamboozle: to delude by the use of such tactics as hoaxing or artful persuasion

[www.thefreedictionary.com]

The Bible has a lot to say about deception.

A: The Who of Deception

Who can be deceived? Answer: Anyone.

Who can do the deceiving? Answer: Others can deceive you and you can deceive yourself (1 John 3:7, Matthew 24:4, or 1 Corinthians 3:18, and Jeremiah 37:9).

Who is the chief deceiver? Answer: Satan (Revelation 18:23, 19:20). He is the father of lies (John 8:44).

B: What Are the Most Common Warnings in the Bible about Deception?

1) Let no man deceive you or watch out that no one deceive you (Ephesians 5: 6, 2 Thessalonians 2:3, 1 John 3:7, Matthew 24:4).

2) Be not deceived (Deuteronomy 11:16; Luke 21:8; 1 Corinthians 6:9, 15:33; Galatians 6:7).

3) Let no one deceive themselves (1 Corinthians 3:18, Jeremiah 37:9).

C: What Are the Main Techniques Used to Deceive People?

1) Lies (Matthew 24:5)

2) Signs and wonders (Matthew 24:24, Revelation 13:14)

3) "By good works and fair speeches" (Romans 16:17 KJV) or "smooth talk and flattery" (Romans 16:17 NIV)

4) Deceivers transforming themselves into apostles of Christ when they are actually deceitful workers (2 Corinthians 11:13)

5) Dressing like sheep to deceive sheep while inwardly they are ferocious wolves (Mathew 7:15)

6) ". . . with every wind of doctrine, by the sleight of men, and cunning craftiness, whereby they lie in wait to deceive" (Ephesians 4:14 KJV) or "by every wind of teaching and by the cunning and craftiness of people in their deceitful scheming" (Ephesians 4:14 NIV)

7) With vain (empty) words (Ephesians 5:6)

8) Through hollow and deceptive philosophy, which depends on human tradition and the elemental spiritual forces of this world rather than on Christ (Colossians 2:8)

9) By any means (2 Thessalonians 2:3)

10) Handling the Word of God deceitfully (2 Corinthians 4:2 KJV) or distorting the Word of God (2 Corinthians 4:2 NIV)

11) In their greed these teachers will exploit you with fabricated stories (2 Peter 2:3).

12) Satan deceives by sorceries (Revelation 18:23) or by magic spell (Revelation 18:23 NIV).

D: What Are the Chief Goals of Deception?

1) To make you turn aside to other gods and worship them

(Deuteronomy 11:16)

2) To lead to wrong path with regard to salvation (2 Peter 2:1)

3) To choke the Word of God out and make it unfruitful (Mark 4:16)

4) To mislead about who will enter the kingdom of God (1 Corinthians 6:9)

5) To mislead about the consequences of sin (Galatians 6:3, 7; Ephesians 5:6)

6) To mislead about the Second Coming of Christ (2 Thessalonians 2:3, Matthew 24: 4–5, 11, 24)

E: What Is the Most Important Thing to Remember about Deception?

1) It is designed so it is hard to catch. As soon as you catch it, it is no longer deception for you.
2) Most deception is clothed with majority truth. The more truth it has the less likely you are to recognize it for what it is.

F: What is the Antidote for Deception? TRUTH.

What is TRUTH? TRUTH is Jesus. Truth is his WORD.

Know what the Word says. Read it for yourself. Do not depend on anyone to conclude for you what the Word says. Go in and study it yourself. Pray to God, and he will help you. If you listen to other people presenting what the Word says, do not take their word for it. Go confirm it yourself. Do not depend on one verse to come to a conclusion about something in the Bible. Look for other verses or sections about the same topic and prayerfully consider them together.

Next, I take each of the techniques used for deception in question B above and add my thoughts on what we need to remember about each. See the table starting from the next page.

Table 1: Techniques used to deceive and points to remember

Techniques used to deceive	Remember therefore	So please consider
1. Lies (Matthew 24:5)	Just because someone says it is in the Bible does not make it true. Just because they give you a verse that seems to suggest something does not mean you run with the verse to justify a practice being taught.	Go study it yourself. Consider other verses on the topic and prayerfully ask God to help you understand what he is saying to you.
2. Signs, miracles, and wonders (Matthew 24:24, Revelation 13:14)	Just because someone displays miracles, signs, and wonders does not make them of God. There are counterfeit miracles, signs, and wonders. Be careful of miracles, wonders, and signs. **THEY WILL be used to deceive, and you do not know when.**	Consider the individual's total lifestyle and whether there is anything in his or her life that could make him or her a wolf in sheep's clothing. Pray. Do not just accept what people do/ say whoever they are! **Never** chase after miracles, signs, and wonders.
3."By good works and fair speeches" or "smooth talk and flattery" (Romans 16:17)	Just because a ministry or person has "good works" does not make it of God. Just because someone talks smooth does not make them of God.	Consider: Are their words based on the TRUTH of the Word of God, or is it mere smooth talk based on **"new ideas"** or **"new revelations"** they have supposedly received?
4. Transforming themselves into apostles of Christ when they are actually deceitful workers (2 Cor 11:13)	Just because a person has a mega church or following or has started many churches or has other "markers of success" does not make them of God.	Consider their lifestyles, their words, and their motivation. Prayerfully consider what they are presenting. Are they after money, profit, and fame in any way? (continued next page)

Techniques used to deceive	Remember therefore	So please consider
5. Dressing like sheep to deceive sheep while inwardly they are ferocious wolves (Mathew 7:15)	Just because someone talks like a sheep (believer) does not make him or her one.	Consider how they showed up on the scene. What is most important in their lives, how do they react under pressure, and how they spend their lives when not in the presence of sheep? Something in their lifestyles will give them away.
6. Every wind of doctrine (Ephesians 4:14)	Just because something is the latest understanding of a scripture or a new way of doing things or a new emphasis on something does not make it of God.	Look between the lines of what is presented. Is the blood of Jesus central? Is Jesus presented as the only way? Is the Word of God given utmost place? Does the Word of God have final say? Is there something people need to do to reach God other than simply accepting Jesus as savior and walking by faith?
7. Vain (empty) words (Ephesians 5:6)	Just because someone is funny, eloquent, has impressive vocabulary, or has new words or phrases or ideas that have been "revealed" to them does not make them of God.	Is freedom from the power of sin through the blood of the cross being presented? How many stories of past success are they giving, and how does this compare to how much of the Word is being presented?
8. Through hollow and deceptive philosophy, (Colossians 2:8)	Just because someone can display impressive play of words to explain an idea from the Bible does not make them of God.	Be careful. Check the Word of God. What God really wants us to know in order to know him and live for him is not complicated. (continued next page)

Techniques used to deceive	Remember therefore	So please consider
9. After the tradition of men, after the rudiments of the world, and not after Christ (Colossians 2:8)	What are the ideas based on? Traditions of men? Is it being recommended because someone says it works or it is a good idea? What is the real source of this idea? Remember deception is not deception unless it is crafted in such a way that you won't be able to tell if you only look at the surface.	You will find many things that are borrowed from other religions or traditions such as Roman Catholicism, New Age, Hinduism, etc. If you research closely and prayerfully, you will know. Do your research.
10. Handling the Word of God deceitfully (KJV) OR distorting the Word of God (NIV) (2 Corinthians 4:2)	What is the agenda in what is being presented? Is it to give you an experience that brings you closer to God? Is it to make you more accepting of other ideas and beliefs? Are one or two verses being used to support a whole teaching/experience? Are you being tricked in any way? Is the Word being distorted to fit the point being made?	Do not chase special experiences. Take God at His word and do not seek further "special experience" to bring him nearer or to take yourself nearer to him. Some of those special experiences are cunningly designed to dupe you into opening yourself up to demonic spirits.
11. In their greed these teachers will exploit you with fabricated stories. (2 Peter 2:3)	Just because a story is well narrated does not make it true. Many are fabricated. Do you sense greed? Are you told there is an element of your faith or life that will improve after you sow a seed into the ministry?	The most important story is as it is written in the Bible. All others can be fabricated. If you are being asked to sow a seed so you can harvest later, beware!
12. By sorcery or magic spell (Rev 18:23)	**Sorcery can produce miracles, signs, and wonders!**	**Do not chase after miracles, signs, and wonders. Many of them will be of Satan, and they will be designed to look legitimately of God to deceive you.**

Please take some time to open your Bible and check out the scriptures I have used in the above Bible study on deception.

In Conclusion

If you consider the verses on deception in the Bible, there are two warnings that comes out very clearly: 1) Let no one deceive you and 2) watch out for deceivers. God entrusts the responsibility to us—to watch out, to take heed, to beware, and to not let anyone deceive us.

Endnotes

Chapter 1

1) http://robinmark.com/the-story-behind-days-of-elijah/

2) *http://en.wikipedia.org/wiki/Fishing_net#cite_note-17*

Chapter 2

(1) http://www.thefreedictionary.com/apostasy
(2) http://www.merriam-webster.com/dictionary/apostasy
(3) https://www.google.ca/webhp?source=search_app&gfe_rd=cr&ei=39gbVeHMAYyzsAe4pIDwDQ&gws_rd=ssl#q=deceived+definition
(4) http://www.merriam-webster.com/dictionary/deceive
(5) Pierce, C, D, & Sytsema, R.W (2001). *The future war of the church. Renew Books, CA, pg 28*
(6) *ibid pg 31*
(7) *ibid pg 74*
(8) *ibid pg 87*
(9) *ibid pg 87/ 88*
(10)*ibid pg 88*
(11)*ibid pg 88*
(12)*ibid pg 95*
(13)*ibid pg 97*
(14)https://pjmiller.wordpress.com/2010/01/15/andrew-strom-urgent-warning/

Chapter 3

1) https://www.youtube.com/watch?v=BCcGaTRwG_4
   and
   https://www.youtube.com/watch?v=xCeVZ6e2T0E

2) https://www.youtube.com/watch?v=2-VIR82MGqE

3) https://www.youtube.com/watch?v=9DM5FmZxBQI
   or https://www.youtube.com/watch?v=983Sx7aZDRE

3.1) https://www.youtube.com/watch?v=I6ZodOrvuUY

4) https://www.youtube.com/watch?v=IlT3oaaed9U
   (watch at mins 36-40 for an example)

5) http://nogodformethanks.tumblr.com/post/76812012105/where-i-live-and-what-i-live-for

6) http://www.huffingtonpost.ca/jessie-golem/leaving-the-church_b_4816252.html

7) https://www.youtube.com/watch?v=eDcAt35IQ5o

8) DeYoung, K., & Kluck, T., (2008) *Why We're Not Emergent: By Two Guys Who Should Be.* Moody Publishers, pg 20-22

Chapter 4

1) http://www.lighthousetrailsresearch.com/blog/?p=13549

2) http://www.gotquestions.org/spirit-guides.html#ixzz3Y2ox6pjz

3) https://carm.org/centering-prayer

4) http://web.archive.org/web/20060825183703/www.christianitymagazine.co.uk/engine.cfm?i=92&id=330&arch=1 and https://www.youtube.com/watch?v=NQiK_hMVC2k

5) http://revivalmag.com/issue/learning-soak-his-love AND http://www.bahaistudies.net/asma/soakingprayer5.pdf for full article

6) ibid

7) https://www.youtube.com/watch?v=WXl4uUi8DUw

8) Dave Hunt and T. A. McMahon, *The Seduction of Christianity* (Eugene, OR: Harvest House, 1984), 123

9) http://www.bahaistudies.net/asma/soakingprayer5.pdf pg 19

Chapter 5

1) Goll, J., (2004). The Seer; The Prophetic Power of Visions, Dreams and Open Heaven. Destiny Image Publishers.

2) ibid pg 34

3) ibidPg 34-35

4) ibid Pg 35-43

5) ibid pg 101

6) ibid pg 125

7) ibid –pg 126

8) ibid pg 126

9) ibid pg 127

10) ibid pg 128

11) ibid –g 55

12) ibid pg 163

13) ibid pg 171

14) ibid pg 171/172

15) Goll, J., (2005). The Lost Art of Practicing His Presence, Destiny Image Publishers

16) Ibid pg 42

Chapter 6

8.1) https://www.youtube.com/watch?v=2_LFpFX_BnA

1) http://catchthefire.com/About/History

2) ibid

3) http://orthodoxinfo.com/inquirers/toronto.aspx

4) http://web.archive.org/web/20050309020450/http://www.niksula.cs.hut.fi/~ahuima/toronto/kundalini.html

5) http://www.bahaistudies.net/asma/torontoblessing2.pdf

6) ibid

7) ibid

8) Strom, A., (2010). *Kundalini Warning: Are False Spirits Invading the Church. Revivalschool publications*

8.1) https://www.youtube.com/watch?v=2_LFpFX_BnA

9) http://www.bahaistudies.net/asma/torontoblessing2.pdf

10) ibid

11) https://www.youtube.com/watch?v=z-QXMGNIVN0 (watch min 1.49-1.53)

12) https://www.youtube.com/watch?v=_KwaFoKq3gM

Chapter 7

1) Goll, J., (2004). The Seer; The Prophetic Power of Visions, Dreams and Open Heaven. Destiny Image Publishers Pg 126

2) Jonathan Welton, in Kris Vallotton, The Physics of Heaven, op.cit,. Kindle location:808.

3) Ibid

Chapter 9

1) http://www.hopeisnowhere.com/resources/new-apostolic-reformation-connection-between-various-leaders/

Chapter 11

1) www.merriam-webster.com and http://dictionary.reference.com/ and [www.thefreedictionary.com]

2) ibid

Made in the USA
Charleston, SC
11 March 2016